Words to Give You Hope

by

Chaplain Randy Elliott

Introduction

In August of 1995 I was injured on the job and taken to the clinic in the small mining town where we lived. My trip to the clinic that day became ten months of being off work and on disability. Just before my disability payments were to run out, the corporation I worked for offered me a new job for about eleven dollars an hour less than what I had been earning prior to my injury. Much to their surprise, I gladly took the job and was happy to get back into the workforce.

My new job was white collar, salaried, at a desk, and required dress attire. This was vastly different from my previous twenty years of employment as an Ironworker, Millwright, Steel Fitter, Mechanic, and Pipe Fitter. With my new job and new surroundings came the realization I was no longer physically able to perform the type of work I had skills for. I had no idea what I would pursue, but I knew whatever it was going to be, I needed to be a much better communicator, especially written communication.

I enrolled in college and hoped to be able to take English 101. I was informed I would be required to take a placement test to assess my written communication skills and I would be placed in the appropriate class based on the results. At that time there were two prerequisite courses prior to English 101. Ultimately the course I needed to complete was College Composition 2 and after taking English 101 there were three prerequisite courses for College Comp 2. If I was unable to test out of any courses I was looking at almost two years of schooling to get where I felt I needed to be with my writing skills.

When I took the test, I was hopeful I would be able to test out of at least one of the prerequisites to English 101. I

1

was horrible in English in high school and it had been eighteen years since I had graduated high school! I was not at all optimistic about the placement test, but I was determined to do my very best. The test consisted of a written essay and I was allowed to choose one of several topics. I do not recall the particular topic I chose, or the required length of the paper, but I was allotted one hour to write and used almost all of it. It would be a week before the results were available.

A few days later the college called to notify me the placement results were in and to set up an appointment with a guidance counselor to go over the test results and decide on a course of action. I was hopeful as I walked into the counsellor's office and wondered if somehow I had qualified for English 101. I sat down, we chatted for a bit, and she informed me I was being placed in College Composition 2! I was stunned, and asked her if she was sure. I sat there nearly in tears and I knew it was all a God thing. Somehow in the eighteen years following high school He had prepared me for this day and this time in my life.

I settled into my desk for the first day of College Comp 2 and looked around the classroom at each of my fellow students. I was obviously the "old man" of the class. Everyone else was in their early twenties and I realized at least most of them had been in college for a couple years or more. They all looked so bright and I began to feel a bit overwhelmed. Here I was a blue-collar grunt for twenty years in a class with a bunch of very smart twenty-somethings. I figured I had once again bitten off more than I could chew and was ready to get up and leave the classroom when the instructor entered the room.

Mrs. Hassel welcomed us, and introduced herself. Then she began to walk us through the course syllabus. All tests, including the final, would be written essays of five to ten pages each. For some of the papers we would be given a short list of topics to choose from, and for others we would be assigned various topics. Mrs. Hassel informed us of the assignments and the date each would be due. The longer she spoke, the more overwhelmed I became. I prayed, "Lord, I'm in way over my head. How will I ever get through this course let alone get any kind of decent grade?" As I finished praying, Mrs. Hassel said something to the effect of, "There will be an assignment date and a due date for each paper. In between these dates you can write and rewrite your paper as many times as you choose. I will grade your paper each time you hand it in and return it to you, and you can rewrite it and turn it in again for grading. You can do this as many times as you like right up until the day it is due." As soon as she finished saying this, my hand shot up in the air. "Would you please repeat what you just said ma'am?" Mrs. Hassel smiled at me and obliged. I said to myself, "I've got this! And I am going to get an 'A' for this course! Thank you, Lord!"

With each assignment I wrote and rewrote the paper again and again until I got one back that had no corrections, and I would turn this paper in for my assignment. I was given an "A" or an "A+" for each assignment. Then came the final, a ten-page paper to be written in class in an hour or less. I would only be able to turn this paper in one time. My only preparation was to go back through all of my rough drafts for the previous papers and read the comments Mrs. Hassel made. I sat down to write the final paper and reminded myself, "God has prepared me for this test, and He didn't prepare me to fail!" I got an A+ for the paper and there was not a single correction or red mark, except for a note at the bottom of the last page that read, "Randy, I have never had a student work as hard as you, and I doubt I ever will

3

again! CONGRATULATIONS! Natalie Hassel." I have been saying it repeatedly over the years since, "Only God!"

I have been writing a weekly newsletter almost since that day. Today this letter is called, "Salt & Light." Over the years I have been told time and again, "You are a really good writer Randy!" Along the way God has crossed my paths with more than a half dozen college English professors who have read Salt & light and commented on my writing ability. These and so many others have repeatedly encouraged me to write books and to put my poems in a book. In early 2020 God slowed me way down and began letting me know I needed to listen to what these people were saying. I understood Him to mean these folks were complimenting His work in my life and I had been blowing it off. A bit later in 2020 God let me know it was time to start writing and publishing books. "Words to Light Your Way" was my first book, and this, "Words to Give You Hope" is my second. Prayerfully others will follow.

I wish to give special thanks to Natalie Hassel and Nancy Rose. I spoke of Mrs. Hassle in the prior paragraphs. Nancy Rose was my Workman's Comp case worker in 1995-1996 and she worked and fought very hard to get me funding for a college education. I would not have been sitting in Mrs. Hassel's classroom had it not been for Nancy Rose. I will be forever grateful to these two ladies for their investment in my life. I wish to somehow one day be able to tell them what their investment became. God bless each of you wherever you may be!

This hope we have as an anchor for the soul,
a hope both strong and secure and one which enters
the Holy of Holies, where Jesus has entered before us having
become our great High Priest forever!

Hebrews 6:19-20 (author's paraphrase)

The Shepherd's Cry

"It is finished!" He cried upon the tree;
Twas the cry of my Shepherd calling to me.

I've a story to tell of He who died; Jesus my Lord, the
Crucified.
He left His glory in heaven above,
to come to earth and show us His love.

He suffered so, as blow by blow;
my sin He paid, His love did show.
He showed His love upon the tree;
as all His blood He shed for me.

"It is finished!" He cried in agony;
My debt was paid, He died there for me.
He rose again from a cold dark grave;
He conquered death, my soul to save.

Now I am His, and in Him safe;
while He in heaven, prepares me a place.
He'll come again from glory on high;
a trumpet and shout, we'll meet in the sky.

"It is finished!" He cried upon the tree;
twas the cry of my Shepherd, calling to me.
"It is finished!" He cried upon the tree;
twas the cry of my Shepherd, calling to me.

John 19:30

No One Like Him

There is no one like Him, nor will there ever be;
He alone is God and always will He be.

Glorify the Lord in His courts with praise;
Fill your hearts with joy and thank Him for His ways.

The Lord is always just, always He is holy;
Come to Him with gladness, and thank Him for His bounty.

He is always good, always good indeed;
By His love and mercy all who come are freed.

His kindness is forever, His grace will never cease;
With His own wherever, eternal life and peace.

He suffered like no other, our sin was His great grief;
He cried out to the Father, His pain bought our release.

He makes known the path of life, in His presence pleasure;
A journey toward no strife, and abundance without measure.

There is no one like Him, nor will there ever be;
He alone is God, forever with Him we'll be!

Luke 7:49

Who is He That

Who is He, that made the trees;
carved the mountains, and sends the breeze?
He is our Maker, making for free!

Who is He, that sends the seasons;
rain and snow and colors pleasin'?
He is our Maker, making for a reason!

Who is He, that created life;
deer and elk and Adam's wife?
He is our Maker, making and alive!

Who is He, that came to earth;
midst angels and shepherds, by a virgin birth?
He is our Maker, making us thirst!

Who is He, that gave His all;
to redeem and save and to us call?
He is our Maker, making for all!

Who is He, that will soon return;
the place prepared, and to us turn?
He is our Maker, making, once spurned!

Who is He, that sets hearts free;
fills with joy, and answers our plea?
He is our Maker, Christ Jesus, making us free!

Mark 4:41

One Day Soon

One day soon, one day soon;
One day soon, He's comin' in the clouds for me.

One day soon, the Son will rise;
From His throne beside the Majesty on High.
It will be, to come for me;
To take me home to His house beyond the skies.

When He comes, all will know;
Most will mourn for the sight of Him, we're told.
But for those who know Him well,
His appearing will be joy that none can tell.

On a white horse, He will ride;
Coming with the host of Heaven by His side.
A trumpet blast, the angel's shout;
Twill be time for His own to come out.

The dead in Christ, the first to rise;
Not to beat us, but to meet us in the sky.
Together we'll see, our glorious Lord;
And realize anew the power of His Word.

Together with Him, we'll live forever;
No more pain, no more suffering, no more, never.
Together with Him, we'll reign on high;
In our home, where sun and moon will never rise.

Forever His, for this He came;
To save a people to be called by His name.
He came and died, and rose again;
One day soon our dwelling place will be with Him!

One day soon, one day soon;
One day soon, He's comin' in the clouds for me.

Mark 14:62

In His Presence

In His presence, He's not far;
Waiting near for you.
Calling out, whispering low;
Only wants you close.

Hear from Him,
Hear from Him;
How else for you to know?

Come to Him,
Come to Him;
Would you know the way to go?

Listen for Him,
Listen for Him;
Ever He calls you near.

Run to Him,
Run to Him;
In His presence is no fear.

In His presence, He's not far;
Waiting near for you.
Calling out, whispering low;
Only wants you close.

Ask of Him,
Ask of Him;
Your best is His to give.

Live for Him,
Live for Him;

Forever you are His.
Go for Him,
Go for Him;
His best is yours to give.

Long for Him,
Long for Him;
One day with Him to live.

In His presence, He's not far;
Waiting near for you.
Calling out, whispering low;
Only wants you close.

Psalm 65:4

Much More Than Just a Man

Hurry, hurry, to bring Him laud;
Son of Man, and Son of God.
Here to earth, with sinners to trod;
Not just a man, but Holy God!

God, He was, forever past;
Man, He became, a Life to last.
Heaven to earth, to walk with us;
Earth to Heaven, to prepare for us!

Sitting now, at the exalted right hand;
'Till the day arrives, when He comes again.
Preparing a place, and interceding is He;
One day in the clouds, He will come for me!

The call from the sky, and a trumpet blast;
He calls for us, He has come at last!
Up in the sky, to meet in the air;
Then off to Heaven, and forever there!

Ear has not heard, nor eye has seen;
What lies in store, for the Lord's company.
No more sorrow, no more tears;
But joy unspeakable, no end to the years!

Hurry, hurry, to bring Him laud;
Son of Man, and Son of God.
Here to earth, with sinners to trod;
Not just a man, but Holy God!

Isaiah 9:6

Vanity

All things, big, and small;
My life would be poorer without them all.
Sunshine and shadows, blue skies and rain;
Even feeling good would be unknown in the absence of pain.
If all were always well, well might be boring.
It is the storms of life that keep us from snoring.
Wellness and pain, sunshine and rain;
If all were the same, all would be vain.

Ecclesiastes 1:2

Return, or No Return

The skies grow dark,
The tide it turns;
Is America really past,
A point of no return?

In God we trusted,
But now we spurn Him;
As if we are clueless,
How desperately we need Him.

For two hundred years,
God blessed and He blessed;
And America stood,
With each passing test.

Two World Wars,
And those of smaller scale;
A beacon for freedom,
Was America's tale.

Now here we are,
In a "bold new age";
Where things that are evil,
Have taken the stage.

As the grass begins to wither,
And the flowers begin to fade;
America grows darker,
And Old Glory cries and waves.

Once powerful and strong,
Such freedom we enjoyed;
But suicidal policies,
And liberal laws we now employ.

The family does not exist,
Without a mother and a father;
There is no great society,
If the family is not proper.

America the blessed,
Land of the free, land that I love;
But America is hopeless,
Without God's Light from above.

Good News is Christ still reigns,
And one day He'll come again;
But will He find in America,
The greatness with which we began?

Our hope is still the Gospel,
The Word of God in human form;
It was freedom to worship God,
For which America was born.

America the beautiful,
Or just a fading glory?
To turn to God or not,
What will be our final story?

Psalm 33:12

Mom

Mom, what does the term conjure up for you?

Mom, she gave us birth in struggle and pain

Mom, she nursed us, cleaned us, clothed us in tireless love

Mom, she hugged us, soothed us, bandaged us
and helped us keep going

Mom, she scolded, paddled, grounded and more,
in hope for a good path

Mom, she fed us, read to us, transported us,
and always hoped the best for us

Luke 2:19

Save Now

Here You come, a riding humbly,
To the cheers and shouts of praise.
On the foal of a lowly donkey,
Offering peace, our souls to save.
Shout "Hosanna!", to the Savior,
Shout "Hosanna!", to the King,
Save now Jesus, the meek and lowly,
Save us now, we humbly sing.

Not a judge, or mighty victor;
Though our freedom is why You came.
Like a lamb led to the slaughter,
For us all, Your life, You gave.
Come now Jesus, bring salvation;
Come to save us from our sin.
Come to die, between two thieves;
Mercy flows now from the tree.

Rise to victory, on Sonday morning;
An empty tomb, the world to see.
Soldiers sleeping, disciples hiding,
Soon to touch, Your hands and side.
Sitting now enthroned in glory,
Making a place for us to dwell.
One day soon, with the host of heaven;
Rides our King, Who comes to save.

Mark 11:9

God Who Loves Me So

You are God who loves me so, You chose me why,
I don't know. You are God who loves me so,
Your grace rains down and
Your mercy flows.

I in sin, You died for me, and shed
Your blood on Calvary. You saved
my soul and You set me free,
so I can live eternally.

You are God who loves me so, and You
made it clear as You took my blows.
My sin all paid, they laid You low, but You
knew no sin, and from the grave You rose.

From the grave You strode in victory,
the stone rolled away, so I could see.
You left this earth to come again,
and You wait for the day at the Exalted Right Hand.

Your grace rains down with new mercy each day;
my joy made full, none can take away.
Each day I live, You walk with me;
and You open my eyes so I can see.

Such love is this that knows no bounds,
lifts me up and never beats me down.
Never to leave, or go away,
pursuing me should I stray.

Your sacrifice made, now our Great High Priest;
interceding each day, as You call to me.
You speak to me, and You call me "friend,"
affirming me in love without end.

You are God who loves me so, You chose me why,
I don't know. You are God who loves me so,
You chose me why, I don't know.

1 John 4:19

The Joy of Sowing

Going and going, with hope filled hearts;
seeking the downcast who need a new start.
Bearing good news, and showing Christ's love;
and offering mercy, His gift from above.

Adventuring along as the Lord leads our way,
seeking the lost each passing day.
Trusting in Him for all that we need; and recalling often,
our sin made Him bleed.

Onward, forward, we must go;
we are the avenue for the lost to know.
Jesus it is the world must meet;
may it be our sacrifice that leads them, to Jesus' feet.

Just a life lived for Him, surrendered and going;
a bag full of seed, and a heart for sowing.
Trusting the Lord to do what He does,
and looking for the day when He will come from above.

The hours are long, and the miles many;
the fields are white, and the harvest is plenty.
One day soon, our reaping done;
we'll see the face, of God's risen Son!

Daniel 12:3

By a Manger Held

He, who by a manger held;
Would one day hold my sin with nails.

He, who on a mother's lap to lie;
Would one day take my sin and die.

He, to whom kings bowed the knee;
Would hold my sin and die for me.

He, who in a manger lay;
Would one day lifeless be laid in a grave.

He, who grew so full of life;
Would one day be my sacrifice.

He, who's birth Heaven proclaimed;
Whose life was such, death had no claim.

He, to one day come for me;
Born in a stable, to die on a tree.

He, the grave no power to hold;
The greatest story ever told.

Luke 2:16

Time to Let Him In

I have Jesus in my heart, He lives inside of me;
He came to make me His, for all eternity.
He died upon the cross, to save my soul from Hell;
The cost of such an act, is beyond what one can tell.

One day He's coming back, for all who've turned to Him;
Oh sinner if you're listening, why don't you let Him in?
If your name's not in His book, for you He will not look;
The gospel story is true, but will He come for you?

In pursuit of you He's been, since first your life began;
Oh sinner if you're listening, why don't you let him in?
He's been calling for some time, someday He'll call no more;
Oh sinner if you're listening, why don't you let Him in?

He's knocking at your door, and calling out your name;
A debt of sin you owe, your debt is why he came.
He gave His life for you, eternal life He gives;
No tomb of His you'll find, forever He does live.

Someday your time will come,
'twill be death that comes to call;
It's because of such a day, that Jesus gave His all.
They'll be no second chance, to be relieved of all your sin;
The time to act is now, why don't you call on Him?

All will come to die, and many will die again;
But death is not the end, for all who come to Him.
Heaven really is, and Hell is just as real;
Jesus offers hope, to whosoever will.

Jesus is the way, to live with God forever;
Any other way, is suffering ever and ever.
The choice is yours to make, before you lie two paths;
Eternity is sealed, the day you breathe your last.

Oh sinner if you're listening, why don't you let Him in?
Oh sinner if you're listening, it's time you let Him in.

Revelation 3:20

The Ultimate Gift

Down from above, He came long ago;
A light in the darkness, His presence did show.

His glory aside, He came as a Servant;
We noticed Him not, too busy to be observant.

He grew up as a shoot, in a very dry place;
He obeyed to the full, He was building His case.

As a boy in the temple, He astounded the learned;
Many years later, by the same He was spurned.

With wood did He work, He sanded and shaped;
Somehow preparation, for the beating He'd take.

Finally the day, His ministry to begin;
He was baptized by John, though never He sinned.

Into the water, He walked Son of Man;
He left on a mission, to die as a Lamb.

He gave and He served, He healed and He raised;
He proclaimed good news, that included His grave?

While praying one night, with His closest three;
Others were plotting, three nails and a tree.

Arrested at night, with torches and swords;
Away He was led, His hands bound with cords.

In a kangaroo court, a conviction was made;
To Pilate He went, a mockery made.

He was taken away, to the Place of the Skull;
Then nailed to His cross, and raised before all.

"It is finished!" He cried, with loud proclamation;
Somewhere in the darkness, the Enemy's celebration.

It wasn't the end, as many believe;
The victory won, from the grave He was free!

He rose from the grave, and ascended on high;
A promised return, on a horse in the sky.

He is coming again, in Glory and Light;
His coming is soon, yes! maybe tonight?

Isaiah 7:14

Shalom!

Whatever the news, this evening gives;
I'll remind myself, that Jesus lives.

I do my best, with the privilege I have;
In hope that America, will last and last.

Either way, my vote counts still;
I did what I could, and made known my will.

This nation wasn't built, on a senate or a man;
Our greatness has been, the God of this land.

We won't ever be destroyed, by an enemy from abroad;
But we may crumble within, if we continue to turn from God.

I hope and I pray, for America this day;
And I'll continue to shout, 'Jesus is the only way!'

At the end of this day, no matter the biz;
It won't change in any way, who Jesus is!

John 14:27

Mercy is Offered

Thanks be to God, for all He has done;
Thanks be to God, for giving His Son!

Mercy is offered, for all to come;
But humility we need, or away we will run!

Oh, come to Christ, by 'the narrow gate';
For the time is now, and the hour is late!

He calls to you, in a 'still small voice',
To turn to Him, is a blessed choice!

'Broad is the road', that leads you away;
So far you will go, you will want to stay!

Jesus calls to you, though His voice seems far;
You can still come home, from wherever you are!

Revelation 22:17

Away in a Manger and Back Again

Did He know born at night, it was also for Him,
to be arrested and sentenced to death by torch light?
One little stable, one lighted candle;
this Baby King, more than most folks can handle.

The world likes to see a babe in a manger,
but a Man on a cross causes such anger.
He hung there for me, and for you too, you know?
And while hanging there, dealt Satan a blow.

Here to earth and out of the womb,
down from the cross and into a tomb.
Into the depths to make proclamation;
away rolled the stone, God's exclamation!

Was He thinking of dying while lying in a manger?
Was He at all aware of the e'er waiting danger?

He came as a Babe, He died as a Lamb;
then up from the grave to the Father's right hand!
He ascended on high after sharing a meal;
while we wait for Him here, He prepares for us still.

He's the light of the world, Savior on high;
draw unto Him, and He'll draw unto nigh.
Creator of all, God's spoken Word,
Giver of Life, our Risen Lord.

Someday He'll return and the world will see,
that He really did die for you, and for me.
We'll go to a home more than any can think;
Could this be the Christmas we move past the brink?

Luke 2:12

Three Nails and No Stones

He came to die, three nails to take;
His joy was full, His sorrow great.

He lived a Shepherd, in search of sheep;
He died a Lamb, His sheep to keep.

He rose a King, with victory in hand;
Empowering His subjects, to take a stand.

Because of our sin, He suffered and died;
'Forgive them Father!', from the cross He cried.

Forgiven we are, who trust in Him;
Forgive we must, 'til He comes again.

He paid the price, and bought our release;
We're avenues of grace, for grace to increase.

As children of promise, with us He begins;
No stones to throw, for we each have sinned.

John 8:8

Faithful and True, is He Calling to You?

Jesus our Savior and High Priest of heaven;
He is our guarantee for God's promises given.
His reign without end, High Priest forever,
Yesterday and today, He changes never!

I read of His name, "Faithful and True";
My life forever His, is He calling to you?

He gives grace for each day, as He watches and prays;
His word He has given, to teach me His ways.
His grace and His word, He gives also His Spirit;
His life to live, and the power to live it!

Interceding is He, at the Father's right hand;
One day He will take me, to the promised land.
Mighty to save, steadfast to love is He;
He is calling today, as He called from the tree!

By His shed blood, my sins are forgiven;
No sin had He, from the grave He is risen!
He's powerful in word, Powerful in deed;
He's powerful to save; and I'm forever freed!

I read of His name, "Faithful and True";
My life forever His, is He calling to you?

Revelation 19:11

A Star to Point the Way

A star in the night, so very big and bright.
Never before seen, drew the attention of kings.

They saddled their horses, gathered a band, and rode
for Jerusalem; to bow before the King of all lands.

Gifts did they bring, fit for a King. To meet Him empty
handed, would be a terrible thing.

Arriving in town, such a stir they did cause.
The news of a Newborn King it was.

The star again appeared to them.
And rested over a humble home in Bethlehem.

The prophets foretold, it was where He would come.
These kings believed, but it is a myth to some.

Finding Him there, alone with His mother;
They bowed to their knees, the gifts they did offer.

Having worshipped before Him,
they went home another way.
Their story still told, around each Christmas day.

Angels we have heard on high;
These wise men knew the reason why.

They worshipped the King who is coming again,
to rule over all from the Promised Land.

What a day it will be, when He finally arrives;
And His praises ring loud, from surrendered lives.

Matthew 2:10

God Who Comes to Me

You are God, who comes to me;
You give me songs, and You hear my plea.
You are God, who comes to me;
God who sees, and comforts me.

You are God who calls me friend;
It is who You are, You love without end.
God who knows, and God who hears;
God who comes, and draws me near.

You are God, there is no other;
God of such love, that You had to suffer.
A friend to me, closer than a brother;
You shed Your blood, my sin to cover.

God of wonders, God of light;
God of power, and O' such might!
God who knows, and understands;
God who stays, and God who mends.

You are God, who comes to me;
Heals my wounds, and sets me free.
God who came, to save my soul;
Forgive my sin, and make me whole.

God who holds my future dear;
Who paid my debt, and calls me near.
You made me new, with no spirit of fear;
You speak to me, and You make my way clear.

You are God, reigning from Your throne;
Rejected by men, yet the Chief Cornerstone.
You are God, who never leaves me alone;
God, who one day, will call me home.

John 4:8

Be Still My Soul

Be still, my soul,
the hour is hastening on.
When here, life will no more toll;
Forever with the Lord, earth's toils forever gone.

When disappointment,
grief, and fear are lost.
Sorrows, forever forgotten;
Love's joys restored, all pain is tossed.

Be still my soul;
When change and tears are past.
All safe, blessed, and whole;
The Savior, to meet at last.

Christ, who holds us dear;
Will one day, draw us near.
All fear is gone, and hope restored;
Shiloh come, and forever, with the Lord!

Psalm 46:10

To Move Forward at Last

Heal my heart, and heal my hurts, dearest Lord Jesus, I pray.
Heal my heart, help me to stand,
that I may move forward this day.

My hurts are deep, and oft' seem past;
Then out spills anger, from a well, that still lasts.

Though not my intent, to hold hurt and get mad;
Twas a thing, came close, and left me sad.

When sad, I be, is when hurt comes to call;
With sadness and hurt, I stumble and fall.

Tis the pain of falling, that makes me angry;
The memory still there; of who it was pushed me.

I don't like the hurts, or how they play out;
But the tape it keeps playing, while I feel such a louse.

It's healing, I need, for my past plagues my present;
The hurt is not who I am, no, it really just isn't.

To deal with my past, and bury it once and for all;
Is the way to move forward, and ever stand tall.

To turn off the tape, seems what I can't do;
So, here I am, Lord; calling on You!

Romans 8:1

Clay in Your Hands

Here I am, Father, waiting and still.
Shape me and make me, after Your will.

Take my heart, Lord, make it wholly Thine.
Mold and remake it, for Your light to shine.
Please take these hands, use them as Your own.
Hold them and make them, to help lead others home.

All that I am, and ever hope to be;
is clay in Your hands, for the molding of me.
Take my life, yielded and still;
make me O' God, after Your will.

Here are my feet, Lord; please make them Yours.
Keep them on the pathway, that leads to celestial shores.

Take my mouth, my tongue, my lips;
anoint them by your fingertips.
Speak through them words of life;
to sooth, to save, to end much strife.

Take my mind, all that is there;
shape it, remake it, after Your care.
Fill it with thoughts of wondrous love;
dreams and themes from glory above.

Here I am, Father, waiting and still.
Shape me and make me, after Your will.

Romans 9:21

He...and Me

Buried, He carried my sin far away;
My sin, far away, forever to stay.
The death of Him, bought life you see;
From the grave, He rose, bringing eternity to me!

My sins all paid, my soul set free;
In bondage to none, His righteousness, my plea.
Done, I am, with life my way;
Far better with Him, and with Him, I'll stay!

Serving Him with gladness, and at times, even sadness;
But life on my terms, a sure formula for madness.
Free, in the center, of His will for my life;
In the eye of life's storm, free from all strife!

Christ Jesus, is He, doing it all for me.
A life to prosper and not to harm;
peace with Him, and no alarm.
Today, to serve Him, in this sin-cursed place;
But, one day, my friend, I will see His face!

John 17:20

Only Jesus Knows

There was a little rabbit, with a fluffy tail.
He liked to hop along, down the bunny trail.
He had four little feet, with a bunch of little toes;
Where he sleeps at night, only Jesus knows.

Only Jesus knows. Only Jesus knows.
Where he sleeps at night, only Jesus knows.

There was a little squirrel, with a fluffy tail.
He liked to climb on high, through the forest veil.
Down the tree for food, here and there he goes;
Where he hides his acorns, only Jesus knows.

Only Jesus knows. Only Jesus knows.
Where he hides his acorns, only Jesus knows.

There was a little girl, with a pony tail.
She liked to hear of Jesus, Jonah and the whale.
She had two special feet, with a bunch of wiggly toes;
What she dreams at night, only Jesus knows.

Only Jesus knows. Only Jesus knows.
What she dreams at night, only Jesus knows.

God did come to earth, it's true and not a tale.
Born in a lowly manger, 'neath a starry gale.
He died upon the cross, for us His mercy flows.
When He's coming back, only Jesus knows!

Only Jesus knows. Only Jesus knows.
When He's coming back, only Jesus knows.

Only Jesus knows. Only Jesus knows.
When He's coming back, only Jesus knows.

Isaiah 11:6

The Glory of Christmas

The glory of CHRISTmas is Christ.
'Twas His glory caused the star to shine bright.

On a night, very dark, and so forlorn;
The king of the land, the Savior he did scorn.

Poor Rachel, who's weeping, would be out of control;
Due to a mad man, and so many lambs ripped from the fold.

One did escape, the most Precious of all;
'Twas the One to be Savior, who would die for us all.

Jesus, His Name, to Egypt did flee;
Just He, His mom, and a man, Joseph; just three.

Then, one day, from Egypt, God called His Son;
Nazareth to go, and much work to be done.

A life mostly obscure, until one day, wine in a glass;
'Twas the start of a chapter, that ended so fast.

Oh!, So many lives, did His life touch!
Then up on a cross, to accomplish so much!

Some, like to say, He came only to die;
But from His cross, "It IS FINISHED!", He cried.

Only three words, but what could they mean;
Cried out by a man, nailed to a beam?

His fate was sealed, or so most thought;
But salvation for many, His blood has bought.

He rose, from the grave, for all to see;
And, for all to believe, and be set free.

He came to us all, in a Bethlehem stable;
In hope, that one day, we will feast at His table!

Matthew 2:11

I Made it All for You

The bees are making honey,
and the trees are bearing much fruit
God's creation showing His handiwork,
and filling our bellies to boot.

His presence He makes known,
His creation testifies,
There is a God who made it all,
Whose home for us is beyond the skies.

The bees do their thing, the chickens and ducks do too;
Through it all the Creator whispers softly,
"I made it all for you!"

The circle of life continues, as the Life-Giver makes it so;
One day He WILL come with the clouds,
to let us know it is time to go.

We'll leave this earth behind, and the best it could ever give,
To go to our forever home, and with Jesus to forever live!

Genesis 2:8

On a Silent Night

On a silent night, the Christ was born,
Into a world so very forlorn.

He came to seek, and to save the lost;
And OH! at such a terrible cost.

His time here began in a Bethlehem stable,
And came to a close, following the Lord's table.

So much there was, the years in between;
So much ahead, as yet, unseen.

Heaven came down to earth below; Why?
Because our Creator God loves us so.

The day approaching, when He will come calling again;
Go tell it on the mountains, and all across the land.

Most will mourn, for the sight of Him;
But for we who are His,
the best CHRISTmas ever, will begin with no end!

Luke 2:7

A Tale of Two Mornings

A tale of two mornings, just two days apart.
One begins very early, while all was still dark.

The other began at dawn's first light,
As the sun burned away, all that was night.

The first followed after the night before,
When a mob, in a garden, dragged God off to court.

The second morning unfolded with an earthquake, and fear.
Signaling to all, that God was still here.

On a morning two days prior, He was nailed to a cross;
His followers ran in fear, believing all hope was lost.

But then, an angel, an earthquake, and fear;
It was the morning that God showed He came to stay near.

Two days earlier, He was buried, and left for dead.
But this day, an empty tomb proclaimed He is risen instead!

One morning, Satan celebrated, thinking victory won.
But this morning, his plans were seriously undone.

One morning, some saw, only a man hung on a tree.
But this morning, a rolled away stone, crying all can be free!

Two mornings, so different, so very long ago.
A story, so great, that all should know!

Luke 24:5

Darkness Past

Crying into the darkness, though the sun be shining bright;
The darkness of a mind, the sun can never light.
Years of anger, hurt, and hatred;
bound by darkness, a life being wasted.

Then one day, the Son to shine;
the light of His word, darkness to find.
First a crack, and then a crevasse;
a mind is opened, and darkness past!

Where once there was anger, now His peace;
Where once there was hurt, now relief.
And hatred that was, is replaced with His love,
As another lost soul grasps Hope, from above!

Mark 5:5

The Peace of Jesus

When the road gets weary and the path seems dark,
Let the Word of God show you the way.
Let the peace of Jesus still your heart,
He promises to care for you each day.

Trust the Lord for that which you cannot know;
He sees the road ahead by which you go.
He will light the way when you follow Him,
And there His very best to you will show.

He has a plan to prosper you and spare you harm.
To provide for you a future and a hope.
He will make the way if you trust Him so,
There's just not a better way to go.

He'll lead you o'er the mountains and through
the valleys low, never to leave you on your own.
He paid a debt for you that He did not owe.
He died and rose in hopes to make you His own.

One day He's coming back to make all things right.
When He does, He wants to take you home.
When the day arrives will you be ready,
or will He pass you by and leave you on your own?

He wants you in His presence and to call you friend;
To know you will be with Him in the end.
He shed His blood for you to make it so,
and there's just no other way to go.

For those who are His own, a place He has prepared.
The day is fast approaching, we'll see each other there.
To live with God forever, giving Him our praise;
Jesus is the one and only Way!

When the road gets weary and the path seems dark,
Let the Word of God show you the way.
Let the peace of Jesus still your heart,
He promises to care for you each day.

John 14:27

By His Hand

Oh glorious day, when I was saved;
The Lord reaching down, to snatch me from the grave!

My life was a mess, the stench made it clear;
But then it was, that the Lord came near!

My sin was great, my shame all the more;
But He, the Savior, my life to restore!

A plan for my life, still He had;
A plan to bless, and make me glad!

"Feed My sheep, and seek the lost;
I'll lead your way, and cover the cost!"

Me, Your witness, and who will listen?
My life's been lived, with sin as my prison!

"Today, My child, I have set you free;
Released you from sin, to follow Me!"

Release me, He did, decades ago;
And made me a testimony, for others to know!

He's leading me still; He's why I still go;
So much to tell, so many must know!

One day, my going will finally be done;
Once again, I will take the Hand of God's Son!

John 8:36

For Becky

Resting in Your presence is he;
where we so much long to be.
Here he battled with sin and strife,
now abundant and eternal life.

Victory here slipped his grasp;
now in Your presence finally clasped.
Forever Yours to fail not again;
but eternal bliss with no end.

Someday a reunion with our friend;
hugs and laughter and joy begin.
In the Savior's presence we will be;
Where cousin Larry found victory!

Luke 23:43

His Family

Jesus loves you, Jesus loves me;
Together we're His family.

He died on the cross, and rose from the grave;
He shed His blood, our souls to save.

Now He's in Heaven, preparing us a place;
One day soon we'll see His face.

Soon He's coming back, on a horse that's white;
To take us home, and make all things right.

Forever with Him, singing His praise;
And knowing His love for endless days.

Jesus loves you, Jesus love me;
Together we're His family!

Ephesians 4:4-6

Home at Last

Life is a "vapor" says the Spirit through James;
We start and we finish, but this is no game.
Each day goes by, the time doesn't last;
Then comes the day, our time is past!

Only one time, we pass this way;
No more chances, not one extra day.
One time through, to get it right;
All live before God, no escaping His sight!

We can live on our terms, if we so choose;
But that IS a game, one only can lose.
Or one can surrender, to Jesus Christ;
And live each day, not fearing the Light!

He is hope, when hope is lost;
To live without Him, just costs and costs.
He allows us freedom, to go it alone;
But He died and He rose, to lead us all home!

We can do it our way, as someone has sung;
But to spare us that hell, Jesus suffered and hung.
Souls are eternal, none comes to an end;
We all must choose, where forever we'll spend!

I made a choice, to receive God's Son;
My life is a race, I am happy to run.
The beginning way back, half a century past;
The finish approaching, and HOME at last!

1 Thessalonians 4:17

So Very Much Alive

Alive, alive, so very much alive;
Jesus paid my debt, for Him alone I strive.
For this He set me free, and to live eternally;
No longer bound by sin, in Jesus I am free!

Jesus set me free, in Him I live each day;
He knows the road ahead, I'll trust Him for my way.
With Him I cannot fail, beside me He will stay;
And though sometimes I stumble, He leads me all the way!

His mercy new each morning, renewed with each sunrise;
Each day He calls me near, to Him my praise shall rise.
He sits beside the throne, of the Majesty on High;
He will not sit forever, soon one day He'll rise!

The day is fast approaching, a white horse He has ready;
There is no time to waste, we must tell everybody.
God did come to earth, the angel announced His birth;
A host sang to His glory, the shepherds told the story!

He lived a perfect life, and died upon a cross;
He paid my debt of sin, I cannot count the cost.
They laid Him in a tomb, and made it real secure;
To them His words lacked power, and never would endure.

In three days the grave was opened,
there was no body there;
Jesus, He has risen for people everywhere.
The stone was rolled away, for all the world to see;
Jesus is the Savior, who died for you and me!

Alive, alive, so very much alive;
Jesus paid my debt, for Him alone I strive.
For this He set me free, and to live eternally;
No longer bound by sin, in Jesus I am free!

John 4:14

Mary Lynn's Prayer

Father God hear my prayer for my treasured friend;
I trust her to You and hold her up for the battle she's in.
Please bless her and keep her and make her strong;
and hold her and speak to her, as You help her along.

I pray, O God, for the effects of chemo to be minimal;
and for her peace and strength to be very maximal.
May You comfort her as she has comforted many;
and may you return to her in this time blessings plenty.

I pray for my friend as she prays so often for me;
that in her time of trial she shines for Your glory.
I hold her up for You to hold so tight;
and pray for her to be healthy with all of my might.

What a blessing she is, my treasured friend;
I pray for a summer of working together again.
When it's all said and done, Your glory we'll see;
and together in June, partners we'll be!

Colossians 1:27

Sittin' in the Shade

Sittin' in the shade I was,
Feeling the tickling of the breeze.
Listening to the sounds I hear,
Is it only rustling in the trees?

No, there is a chirping sound,
Perhaps a cricket, or a bird.
Maybe a lost little penguin,
But how absurd!

I hear a sound like creaking,
It seems to be quite distant.
A rusted gate, a swaying branch,
I ponder, exactly "what is it?"

Another sound it seems is drawing near.
I heard the same sound yesterday, and now it is quite clear.
Tis the sound of hopes and dreams,
and things I cannot borrow.
I can only wonder what's in store for me,
with the coming of tomorrow?

Isaiah 55:12

Bluest Sky

I was riding up a dusty draw
'Neath the bluest sky I ever saw;

In the draw were lots of flowers
I could have stayed for hours and hours.

The trail grew steep,
The sun grew hot;

A cowboy I am,
This is my lot;

I ride the trails, through these draws
Then sit and write of what I saw

John 1:1

A Cowboy's Boots

A cowboy loves his boots,
They make him howl and hoot

He wears them with his suits,
He wears them when he shoots.

A cowboy loves his boots,
They help him ride and scoot.

A cowboy loves his boots,
They make him howl and hoot.

He wears them for hours and hours,
I hear some do even in the shower.

A cowboy loves his boots,
They help him work the chute.

A cowboy loves his boots,
They make him howl and hoot.

He usually has several pair,
His favorites show the most wear.

A cowboy loves his boots,
Some are even colored like fruit

John 1:27

Oh Happy Day!

Oh happy day,
When the Christ child was born;
In a humble manger
Lay God in Human form.

On earth was man,
By sin so very torn
Among them was Joseph,
Crushed emotions and feeling forlorn.

In a quandary he was
Until the angel came,
Take Mary with child
Give the baby, Jesus the Name.

Quite certain the angel's
Words were true,
Mary he took to himself
And her baby boy, too.

Nine months Joseph waited
For nine months was he berated;
Steadfast he held to the Word of God
Then off to Bethlehem they trod.

No room to be found
On a cool dark night,
Until finally a stable
With dim candlelight.

Then into this world
The God-Man came,
A boy named Jesus
Joseph gave Him the Name.

He grew like a shoot
A root from dry ground;
One day in the temple
A wise crowd to confound.

With hammer and nails
He humbly served His own,
In a simple carpenter's shop
Perhaps working mostly alone.

His hands were splintered
From the wood that He shaved;
Was it a constant reminder
Of all that He gave?

A carpenter's "Son"
He lived to die;
When His work was finally complete
"It is finished!" He cried.

Oh happy day!
When the Christ child was born
The Savior for all
'Twas God in human form!

Luke 2:20

Burdens

Life's burdens are many,
and they often get stacked;
But the Lord didn't create us
for bearing burdens on our backs.

"Cease striving!" says He;
and "Know that I AM God!"
Bring your burdens to Me,
and freely may you trod.

It's hard to move forward,
when all strength is needed just to stand;
Soon the load begins to crush,
as burdens can only demand.

Weak and heavy laden,
as if our feet have turned to lead
Unable to go to Him,
He comes to us instead!

1 Peter 5:7

He Holds Me

By His wounds my healing came;
He bled for me and took my shame.
His mercy flows still today;
My sin He paid, and washed away.

He took my life and made me His own;
He redeemed the years that I had blown.
He made me new on His potter's wheel;
A vessel for honor, and doing His will.

He holds me today, as He did long ago;
My life all His, His grace still flows.
The road ahead, I knowest not;
But in His hands, He holds my lot.

Someday He'll come to take me home;
Someday I'll bow before His throne.
Someday in Heaven, when I view my past,
I'll see all the ways He held me fast.

John 17:24

Almost Home

Into this world naked and screaming,
Crying and flailing and grabbing for breath,
No dreaming or scheming but destined for death;
Already was I on my way home.

Lessons to learn and bridges to burn,
Which way to go, which way to turn?
Off to school for "education",
nothing there of eternal salvation.
Unknown to me, I was on my way home.

Life an accident, could it be true?
So much to learn, if only I knew!
Lots to know and so far to go,
not knowing where, I ran to and fro.
But guided I was, and on my way home.

The opposite way, that's where I went.
In the wrong direction, I went and I spent!
Further and further, away I did wander,
The Savior pursued, calling me yonder;
"This is the way, My child, come home!"

So far away, so much forgotten, life was miserable;
and me? I was rotten.
The Savior pursued, still calling my name;
"I died for you, and even your shame!
Hello, Hello!, where did you go?
Come unto Me, and I'll lead you to home!"

I answered, I turned, and changed my direction;
I responded, pursued, and took up the chase!
T'was Jesus who called from a much better place!
"Come on, Come on! this way is home!

It's fifty years later since first I began,
I crawled, I walked, I stumbled, and fell;
Eventually no stumbling, I started my running.
So very far, I ran the wrong way;
Finally the Savior, He caught me one day!
And taking my hand, He turned me for home.

Half a century has passed, perhaps decades to go;
Once running and lost, but pursuit now I know.
The Savior who called me, chased me and caught me;
Now waits for me yonder, and I'm almost home!

1 John 3:2

Resolved to Run

In my weakness and my failures,
You are so merciful to me.

You hold all my future days to come;
Yes, You hold each and every one.

You alone are my all in all,
And all the more so when I fall.

You stand me up, but not too tall,
And hold me there, lest I continue to fall.

There is no shadow of turning with Thee,
Least of all, to turn away from me.

You draw oh so close to me,
To keep me very near to Thee.

You take me to where I could never go;
Yes, it's true, You love me so.

Apart from You, I have no hope;
Away from You, I am so limited to cope.

Life is filled with many, many risks,
Risks that often cause my life to twist.

You hold all my future days to come,
In all my days I am resolved to You to run.

Proverbs 18:10

Out of Eternity

From eternity past, the Word of God came,
To the womb of a teen, who's life, never to be the same.

Creator God, who spoke all into being,
Is the Babe in the manger, and at Mary's breast feeding.

The Creator of life, created the young woman
Who would carry and birth, in one body, God and Man.

From eternity past, to the present He came,
This God-Man Jesus, to cover our shame.

In blood He was born, and bleeding He died;
As He hung on the cross, "It is Finished!" He cried.

A story that was written, in eternity past,
Carried out to perfection, as the Savior breathed His last.

From eternity future, He will come again,
Away, Away! we will go with Him!
At last, at last! our eternity begins!

John 8:48

Lamb of God

O' Lamb of God, sweet Lamb of God;
I love You, Holy, Lamb of God.
Oh wash me in Your precious blood,
Til I am just a lamb of God.

Your only Son, no sin to hide;
But You have sent Him, from Your side,
To walk upon, this guilty sod;
And to become the Lamb of God.

Your gift of love, they crucified;
They laughed and scorned Him, as He died.
The Humble King, they named a fraud;
Then sacrificed the Lamb of God.

O' Lamb of God, sweet Lamb of God;
I love You, Holy, Lamb of God.
Oh wash me in Your precious blood,
Til I am just a lamb of God.

I was so lost, I should have died.
But You have brought me to Your side,
to be led by Your staff and rod;
And to become a lamb of God.

Apart from You, my life a mess.
Still You pursued me nonetheless.
To walk the path, Your son did trod;
And prove to be a lamb of God.

O' Lamb of God, sweet Lamb of God;
I love You, Holy, Lamb of God.
Oh wash me in Your precious blood,
Til I am just a lamb of God.

One day soon, You'll come for me;
My sins all paid, a soul set free.
You'll raise Your scepter, once a rod;
And welcome home this lamb of God.

O' Lamb of God, sweet Lamb of God;
I love You, Holy, Lamb of God.
Oh wash me in, Your precious blood;
'Til I am just a lamb of God.

My Jesus Christ, the Lamb of God.
My Jesus Christ, the Lamb of God.

(The authors for half the song are anonymous;
The rest is written by the author)

John 1:29

Someday

Someday, the Savior will call,
Someday, the gates will open,
Someday, to realize all that He has spoken.

Someday, this life will pass, the Universe rolled up as a scroll,
Someday, time to be no more, and death no more to toll.
Someday, a brand-new body, to be youthful as a foal.

Someday, sin forever gone, corruption to be no more,
Someday, to finally realize, all of Heaven's store,
Someday, the day to come, we've all been waiting for.

Someday, to see the Savior, face to face and be as He,
Someday, no effects of sin, and to be forever free.
Someday, the full reality, of why Jesus died for me!

Revelation 21:4

He Is

He cares, He cares, He really does;
but He never sends up flares.
He needs no help, reinforcements, or advice.
He only needs for us to rest our hearts in Him.
He is the Peace that answers our grief.
He is the Comfort that gives us relief.
He is the Love that answers our loss.
He is the Hope that squashes our despair.
He is the Presence that dispels our loneliness.
He is the Strength that keeps us going.
He is the Grace to see us through.
He is the Guide who knows the way before us.
He is the Sovereign who holds our future.
He is the Shelter that hides us in the storms.
He is the Captain who steers us to safe and good places.
He is the Lion that faces our enemies and accusers.
He is the Shepherd who leads us to situations of rest.
He is the Savior who sets us free.
He is the Embrace that holds us close.
He is the Heaven that draws ever more near.
He is the King who comes to take us home.
He is the God of all our circumstances.
He is the Lord who answers to nobody.
He is!
He is!
He is!"

Hebrews 1:3

Always There

So many hearts are suffering,
so many have experienced loss;
It is for the hurting and the guilty,
Jesus suffered so on the cross.

Sin, the curse, the pain,
and the eternal cost of it;
Jesus shed His precious blood,
to pay for, heal, and cover it.

One only needs to call on Him,
in the midst of one's despair;
If one seeks Him, one will find Him,
for Jesus is always there.

Isaiah 61:1

Seasons

Summer is winding down, and fall is winding up;
The geese are flying, the leaves slowly turning,
as we move from season to season.

A time for everything, a wise man once said,
and Creation backs it up;
The seasons of nature, the seasons of life,
and perhaps even a season for reason.

Tumultuous times, these days we live in,
so many reasons for looking up;
To follow His path, narrow way and gate,
and finally the season is Heaven.

Hebrews 12:2

A Plan for the Ages

A plan was formed
In ages past
Before our world was made

God's glory to show
Through His mercy and grace
In a way never before displayed

A key to this plan
Was the failure of man
An eternal cost to be paid

Man did fail
Through fault of his own
The cost for his sin was laid

Hell once ready
For Satan and his own
Now open to any who will pay

But God sent His Redeemer
To be born of the virgin
No wages for sin to be weighed

He lived for the record
A life that was perfect
And readied a ransom to be made

Slaves to sin
All were we
Death the wages to be paid

Along came Jesus
God's perfect Lamb
On a cross built for us was He layed

He died there as planned
In ages way back
To God's presence He opened the way

His sacrifice made
He rose from the grave
Our sin in the full was paid

He lives to save
All who will come
God's grace so grandly displayed!

Ephesians 1:4

The Last Bell Tolls

Rolling thunder, crashing lightning,
much around us could be easily frightening
But there sits the King, calm on His throne;
nothing to Him is ever surprising.

His plans go forth, no one can hinder them,
leading up to the day when He will come hither;
Oh! For today that He might come,
but what of the lost souls left to be tinder?

My heart longs for the day when we'll meet Him in the air;
hope fully realized in His care;
My heart longs also for the lost to be saved,
so many headed for a Christless forever.

So glad it's not I, but the Lord in control,
in His Sovereign time the last bell tolls'
Sorrow behind when this day comes,
joy unspeakable if our name is on His roll.

1 Corinthians 15:24

Thankful Praise

I thank God for a body still mostly strong
I praise God for being a Saviour
Who forgives me all my wrongs.

I thank God for the days when the sun shines bright,
I praise God for His presence
when nothing seems right.

I thank God for the sense to know right from wrong,
I praise God for His patience
when my sense doesn't last long.

I thank God for the nights when my body can rest,
I praise God for His comfort
when my mind is stressed.

I thank God for the days He gives as I take each breath,
I praise God for His guidance
for His footprints to direct my path.

I thank God for a day future when I get to go home,
I praise God for His hand on my shoulder
while still here on earth I roam.

1 Thessalonians 5:18

All Equal

We've a message to share,
that ALL humanity matters,
From those still in the womb,
to those whose lives are in tatters.

God cares most about people,
the old and the young,
He loves us all so much,
that He gave us His Son.

We're all equal there,
at the foot of His Son's cross,
Color and age do not matter,
He came for the lost.

"Lost" has no color,
and nothing to do with appearance;
Jesus' cross is the way,
for all to come to God without interference.

Galatians 3:28

Privileged to Tell

We get to tell His story,
to the desperate and lost,
How came and gave His all,
to redeem us at such cost!

The price of sin incalculable,
yet covered by His blood on a cross
Not a plan of earthly origin,
but a heavenly plan to save the lost.

Sometimes we get to charge,
sometimes we get to wait;
The timing is the Lord's,
and our sharing is never, ever, late.

The cost of our redemption,
so astronomically high;
So many have yet to hear,
and the question here is, "Why?"

2 Corinthians 5:20

Story Time

The work is too great for one,
the worker must be backed by many;
Without a team of partners,
the worker reaches very few, if any.

To enter the "fields" is a privilege,
even when done from a desk;
But it is the prayers and gifts of a team,
that make way for folks to be blessed.

One day we'll all be together,
with the Master who made it all happen;
Oh! the stories to tell and hear,
of what the Master did when we listened.

1 Corinthians 3:8

The Lord Will Come

Someday the Lord will come,
His justice to reign at last;
Injustice, unfairness, calamities, and violent protests,
will be forever past.

Someday the Lord will come,
all tears to wipe away;
No sorrow, no pain, no suffering, no fear;
all will pass when comes His day.

Someday the Lord will come,
such relief His appearing will be;
With new bodies where all is right,
in His eternal presence forever we will be!

Revelation 1:7

Heaven's Perfect Lamb

He arrived in a manger two thousand years ago;
A star announced His coming, and set a few hearts aglow.

The shepherds heard the news, 'neath a cloudless sky that night;
as the angels soon departed, they hastened to the site.

A stable and a manger, a woman and a man;
wrapped in cloths on linen, lay Heaven's Perfect Lamb.

The shepherds entered in, looked and bowed in awe;
then spoke with great joy, of all they heard and saw.

The shepherds went rejoicing, perhaps skipping to the sheep;
while Mary held a baby boy, who soon was fast asleep.

The years went by, the child grew, and soon He was a man;
Mary watched it all and wondered, "How is He the Perfect Lamb?"

He made water into wine, at a feast in Galilee.
The servants wondered as they poured, "Who can this Maker be?"

He caused the lame to walk, the deaf to hear,
and made the blind to see.
He spoke the Word of Truth to men, to set the captives free.

He soon became the "captive", accused of blasphemy.
Cursing, spitting, beating, lashing;
then to carry His own tree.
Forgiving, loving, living, dying; this Christ of Calvary.

A star, an angel, shepherds, a manger;
a cross, a tomb, who is the Stranger?

A catch, a meal, and words to restore;
then up with the clouds, till seen no more.

Someday on the clouds, a white horse and its Rider;
a trumpet and shout, call those He is after.

The place prepared, He comes for His own;
and takes us with Him, to our heavenly home!

Revelation 7:17

Wedding Day

Oh happy day,
You two are one;
A new road ahead,
You have now begun!

A life to live,
And a family to grow;
Many years before you,
With children in tow!

Good things to find,
As you make your way;
May blessings be yours,
With each passing day!

Matthew 19:5

Conception

Conception is the point,
all human life begins;
What's to be "conceived",
if nothing changes within?

All human life matters,
mankind alone breathes the breath of God;
It was His breathing into Adam's nostrils,
that put us on the earth to trod.

One can look at other humans,
and keep doing as one pleases;
Better is to look at one another,
and see the face of Jesus!

Psalm 139:13-14

Oh, to Bow Before Him

Oh, to be Mary, and hold Him.
Oh, to hear, and behold Him.
Oh, to bow, before Him,
Christ, the Lord.

Jesus was born in Bethlehem, A long, long, time ago.
But long before the manger scene,
He reigned Eternal King.
God, He was, who came to earth,
The virgin gave Him birth.
Fully God, He did remain;
Redemption is why He came.

He caused a stir, and scared a king;
Peace on earth to bring.
The shepherds heard, and sought the Babe,
Who in a manger laid.
They told of all they saw, And the news the angels gave.
Who'd have thought the King of kings,
To be born in a Bethlehem cave?

Oh, to be Mary, and hold Him.
Oh, to hear, and behold Him.
Oh, to bow, before Him;
Christ the Lord.

Eight days old, Simeon saw,
God's salvation plan;
The baby King of Holy birth,

would be God's perfect Lamb.
The wise men came from a country far,
only His star was seen.
Finding Him on Mary's knee,
they bowed to the newborn King.

His parents feared the wrath of Herod,
to Egypt they did speed.
It was foretold, from Egypt He'd come,
to be the Nazarene.
God did come to the earth He made,
and in a manger lay.
Who'd have thought salvation won,
by a Babe on Christmas Day?

He reigned eternal, forever past;
And, He'll reign forevermore.
One day soon, He'll come for us;
To show us what's in store.
Who'd have thought, salvation won;
By a Babe sleeping on the hay?
God, He was, who came to earth;
To be born on Christmas Day.

Oh, to be Mary, and hold Him.
Oh, to hear, and behold Him.
Oh, to bow, before Him,
Christ, the Lord.

Matthew 2:11

To Be a Blessing

Oh, to be a blessing, to Him who is most blessed;
To know His heart is filled with joy,
as we follow Him with each step.

To bless the heart of God,
what possibly could be more fulfilling;
To hear His voice, as He guides our steps,
and be faithful in our following.

To bless His heart in worship,
each and every day
As we follow in His footprints,
all along the way.

Lord, help us to be a blessing,
to You first of all;
Knowing when we do so,
we will always hear You when You call!

John 14:15

A Nation to Celebrate

A nation without borders,
is a nation that will not be;
A nation that forgets it's past,
is a nation that will be history.

May our flag, Old Glory, continue to fly
To the sound of The Star Spangled Banner,
that helps us remember why.

We're still a nation to celebrate,
so much in our past is good;
Stories of great men and women,
their stories to tell we should.

The negatives need told the same,
nothing changes if we cover the shame;
Lessons of history need taught and learned,
or lose our way and repeat the same.

Wars were fought,
so many gave;
A nation to be known,
as the land of the free and home of the brave!

Psalm 144:15

Hastening the Day!

The days grow dark,
as storm clouds rise,
Lawlessness is growing,
"forget the past!" is the cry.

Such a heritage,
God has blessed us all with;
So much being spoken
as truth today is lies or myth.

Many have suffered,
no question there;
We're all in this together,
dark skin or fair.

One race we are,
to walk this earth,
But Oh! the separation,
for lack of the second birth.

Jesus is the answer,
and His is the best way;
We must live as heavenly spirits,
and do all to hasten the Day!

2 Peter 3:12

Out of Chances

Chaotic times we live in,
it is really nothing new;
Though it may have been awhile,
humanity portrays a zoo.

If you teach kids they are just animals,
should a zoo portrayal surprise?
To our downfall we turn from God,
evolution will be our demise.

Racism is a byproduct,
only possible if we evolved;
Created in the image of God,
but believing lies we devolve.

Spiraling out of control we are,
as technology advances;
God desires us to turn to Him,
soon, before we run out of chances!

2 Corinthians 6:2

Always He is Doing

Our God is ever watching, listening, doing,
even when it seems it isn't so;
So hard sometimes to sit and wait,
while we wonder what we have yet to know.

But this is always certain, God is in control,
watching, listening, and doing;
His silence often befuddling, His providence mind boggling,
always He is doing.

His ways are not our ways, we can give Him praise for that,
And when it is all said and done,
we'll praise Him all the more, as we look back!

Psalm 121:3

We Wait

We wait, and wait, and wait,
for so many things that take too long;
The desire to possess what we are waiting for,
often seems so strong.

Time always moves so slow,
when relief or pleasure is the goal,
But then it moves so very fast,
when we want it to pass by slow.

To wait for things that matter little
is really quite trivial;
To hope for things that matter much
is surely a much better deal.

We hope for what we cannot see,
but Oh!, we know it is so real;
One day the King is coming back,
and Heaven our wait will fill!

Romans 8:24-25

Giver of Life

The perils of life are many,
and most beyond our control;
But the Giver of life watches over,
and sustains us beyond life's toll.

The toll of life eventually catches us all,
none of us exits alive;
But the Giver of life is there for us,
snatching us from death to His side.

The trials of life are many,
and so many bumps on our way;
But the Giver of life goes with us,
and we ride the bumps with Him each day.

The time will come for us each,
for our earthly ride to end;
But the Giver of Life will be waiting,
and our eternity with Him will begin!

Isaiah 41:10

Living Each Day

Living each day, one day at a time;
Experiencing God's creation,
and seeing His glory Divine.

To sing His praises throughout the day,
As we rest in His presence,
and trust Him with our way.

He leads us on good paths
as through this life we go,
And shelters us with His care
when life throws us to and fro.

We plan our days, as we need to;
He directs our steps, as only He can do.

His care is always present,
no matter where we are;
One day He'll come to take us,
to His place beyond the stars.

Matthew 6:34

Never Slow

The Lord is never slow,
nor ever in a hurry;
Time is nothing to Him,
in spite of all our worry.

"If only You had been here!"
someone once said to Him,
Not knowing who He really is,
nor that He has always been.

He cares for every detail,
and knows the number of our hairs;
He sees, He cares, He really does;
but He never sends up flares.

For me, I know all these things,
but still wish He'd hurry up;
For Him, He knows all of me,
and waits for me to catch up!

John 11:21

Change

Waiting and waiting,
for things to change;
like watching paint dry,
or a stopped sink to drain.

The harder you wait,
the slower change gets here;
Getting worked up and frustrated,
well, you might lose more hair.

Might as well make the most,
of the extra time you've been given;
Making the most after all,
is what makes livin' really livin'.

One can wait for the change,
in hope things will be better,
Or one can stay busy,
and not be a fretter.

One thing is certain,
when it is all said and done,
Forever change will happen,
the day we see the Son!

1 John 3:2

Hope Has Life

There was a day,
the sky turned black;
Hope seemed lost,
and folks talked smack.

A body hung, lifeless, and bleeding;
Was this really the same One,
so many He had been feeding?

In triumph, He lived,
in shame He did die;
They that mourned Him,
left asking, "Why?"

Two days passed,
and the Son rose again;
In Him hope has life,
and eternity begins.

Many are those,
mocking Him still;
But in Him, is new life,
for whosoever will!

John 4:14

Believing You Will Come

In these days, when skies seem black,
Sin running amuck, and Creation out of whack.

Our sins are glaring, we turned our backs,
And here we are again, humanity under attack.

Science! Science!, seems to be our cry;
Tis the cry of the lost, as Your Name we deny.

But there are those, perhaps many,
who know who You are;
For those You have made righteous,
won't You come from afar?

We look to You, Lord, believing You will come,
Be it to stop this virus, or be it our days are done.

1 Thessalonians 4:16

Sonrise

The glory of the Lord will shine,
with the SONrise from on high;
A day is fast approaching,
when all darkness will forever hide.

The trumpet of the Lord will sound,
and His shout from heaven will come;
It will be the sound of joy untold,
as He calls us all together as one.

Joy unspeakable awaits us,
in the glorious Light of His presence;
For now we tread His earth below,
while He prepares our eternal residence.

One day the Son will rise,
even now He is at the ready;
We march on toward our heavenly home,
His presence keeping us steady!

Luke 1:78

Promise of Better Days

In days of old, God sent the hornet,
to drive enemies away;
But in present times, He sends the bee,
the promise of better days!

There once was a day, the sky turned dark,
and the Savior breathed His last;
But then a day, the Son shown bright,
and the Savor did come back!

A day is coming, fast approaching,
when for many better days will be no more;
But on that day, for we who know Him,
the Savior will open Heaven's door!

Trials are present, and will be again,
and the fields are ever white;
These are the days, to know the Savior,
and forever change one's plight!

For we who know Him, the joy of telling,
in hope for others to be set free;
Oh! If they will only respond,
and be spared a Christless eternity!

Revelation 1:7

His Purposes are Best

In perilous times we live,
we the body of Jesus;
Our lives are in His hands,
for Him to do as He pleases.

Sometimes we have to suffer,
to identify more with He;
Surrender to His will,
or one can always flee.

To a cross He once surrendered,
as He hung for you and I;
When peril comes our way,
we must look to Him, and not deny.

Believing that He cares, and His purposes are best,
And that one day in His presence,
we will find our perfect rest!

Isaiah 55:8

A Time Will Come

Funny what the Lord will use
to bring people to their knees;
Trials of life, health scares too,
or things invisibly floating on the breeze.

Never our pain, or struggles,
or even weakness He likes to see;
Just longing for hearts, turned toward Him,
and hearts forever set free.

A time will come, for all things to unravel;
it will be the beginning of the end;
But along the way, the coming King, arrives
for those whose knees did bend.

So many people, so many struggles,
so little time to spend;
But for all who bow, and turn to Him,
a glorious future, forever without end!

Revelation 22:5

The Journey

Long the journey is,
and sometimes very trying;
But God is ever with us,
that there is no denying!

Such a journey life can be,
as the road unfolds before;
But the Master of the way ahead,
knows all that is in store!

Times and seasons come and go,
as we continue on the way;
As the Master of the way ahead,
proves to be Master of each day!

Someday the journey on earth be past;
But our journey with the Master will forever last!

Hebrews 13:5

Grace, Grace

Grace, grace, God's grace,
to set souls free, from the prisons they're in;
Grace, grace, God's grace,
amazing and powerful, when released within.

Grace, grace, God's grace,
to set souls free, new lives to begin;
Grace, grace, God's grace,
wonderful and peaceful as the battles end.

Grace, grace, God's grace,
still saving souls from the rages of sin;
Grace, grace, God's grace,
prison doors opened, as His Spirit comes in.

Grace, grace, God's grace,
let it reign, let it reign, let it rain, that storms will end;
Grace, grace, God's grace,
to calm raging seas as the Son speaks in.

Amazing grace, how sweet the sound,
that saves prisoners...like we;
Amazing grace, how sweet the sound,
His voice still saying, "Come unto Me!"

John 1:16

To Rise Together

Together, forever, as only God can do;
The motley church I have on the inside,
together with all of you!

One day, to rise together,
to meet Jesus in the air;
The time is still a mystery,
but the place we'll go is forever there!

Oh my! One day a trumpet blast,
and then His voice will call;
It will be His coming,
for us one, and for us all!

Our work on earth be done,
His fold with no more room;
He's come to take us home,
and seal forever Satan's doom!

1 Thessalonians 4:17

Well Done!

In the midst of all life's trials,
and battles that often ensue,
There is the sound of His so sweet voice,
"I have my eyes on you!"

No, He never forgets,
those who are His own;
The trials are preparation,
for the day He will take us home.

Tis one thing most He wishes to say,
when the things of earth be gone;
It is the reason for trials today,
the "Well done!" that is to come!

Matthew 25:21

Good Plans

Fiery ordeals will come our way
As we live our lives in Christ each day.

Trials are not fun, in fact, they stink,
But God's hand is evident if we slow down and think.

Good things, somehow, are in the midst;
It is God always doing to make the situation fit.

Good plans, He has, for you and for me;
Plans that will bless us today, and for eternity!

Jeremiah 29:11

Captives, You and Me

One day a trumpet sound,
to gather us on high;
Comes the Master for His sheep,
and no one can deny.

From the corners of the earth,
a few great, and many not;
All His own will come,
not one will be forgot.

He calls us each by name,
but a new name each will be given;
A name to speak of His work,
and His shaping us for Heaven.

His promises all fulfilled,
and the captives all set free;
And among them in the crowd,
captive you, and captive me!

John 10:28

King Jesus

It's all about Jesus, this thing the Christian life
The King who will one day come,
and put a forever end to strife.

All about Jesus when life is good,
all about Jesus when life gets rough,
All about Jesus when life's not fair,
and being like Jesus can be kind of tough.

He is the King of ancient days,
and King of eternal life, always.

King who will one day come again,
King with Whom forever, never ends!

1 Timothy 6:15-16

Handful of Seeds

Going and going, as Jesus commands;
Sowing His Word wherever it lands.

Knowing not always, for what or for whom,
But going and sharing, in hope the seeds bloom.

Hearts made ready, as only God can do,
Receiving His Word, and growing roots too.

A handful of seed, a plethora of soils
Some pray, some give, some sow, and together we toil.

The work is the Lord's, He offers us a part
The doing is all His, right from the start.

Luke 8:15

Gospel is Our Hope

The end is coming, for life as we know
There will be a day, for the Universe
to be rolled up like a scroll.

It may be soon, or a ways down the road,
Jesus says "Come!" to be relieved of your load.

Wide is the gate and broad the road
that lead to destruction;
If we don't turn back soon
it will be the demise of such a great nation.

The Gospel is our hope, or we've no hope at all;
To go and go and share, is still our Master's call.

"I'll shout it from the mountain top
I want my world to know
The Lord of love has come to me
I want to pass it on." (Kurt Kaiser)

Matthew 12:21

The Word Became Flesh

The Word became flesh, how amazing it is,
The God of Creation would visit a place like this

And visit He did, more amazing still,
He came in the form of a man, after God's will.

Some say it is impossible for a man to become God,
They are right of course,
but God became man, this earth to trod.

He came to be one of us, remember,
He *came* from heaven above,
His coming to us wouldn't leave us the same.

Once a people without hope, now Hope lives for us
In between was the cross, where Just died for unjust.

Forgiveness is offered, through His shed blood on the cross
To reject such an offer, results in eternal loss.

The Word became flesh, for us to live with Him
He did all that was needed, for eternal life to begin!

John 1:14

His Handiwork

The work of His hands, you're special, you know
Before your conception He already knew,
and as one weaves a tapestry, He began to sew.

Knitted you together, there inside your mother's womb
An egg to be fertilized, and a blossom to bloom.

As life nourished life, you began to grow
All the while you were growing, as a person to know.

Knitted together, there in limited space
And knitted specifically, made for a place.

Outside to begin, abruptly in strife
Knitted together to begin, this journey called life.

Psalm 139

Deserving of Wrath

Born into sin, everyone, everywhere
Each hopelessly lost, does anyone care?

Created by God, in His likeness it's true
Yet deserving His wrath, sinners me and you.

Hopelessly lost, and eternally damned
God sent forth His Son, to be our Perfect Lamb.

Not His wrath He holds out to us, but His mercy instead
Mercy bought for us by God the Son, on a tree, dead.

Death was not final, but in victory risen and alive again
His triumph over death, means we can have life without
end.

To love Him is a choice, our choosing Him is not guaranteed
To create us with no choice, would have made us not free.

Lost in our sin, to be free comes at such cost
God loves us so much, He'd rather die than see us lost.

Ephesians 2:3

To the End

It is the trials of life, that shape us most
If we can just persevere, and not become toast.

There are times on life's road, when it gets really tough
We must put our heads down, and bull our way forward,
no matter how rough.

Praise God for our Savior, Who sees our days
And walks right beside us, each step of our way.

When the way gets weary, and hope wears thin
He's there with His strength, to carry us through to the end.

Matthew 28:20

No Sin to Hide

God sent His Son, no sin to hide
Nothing to keep covered, His life open wide.

He lived His life with purpose,
perfectly fulfilling His Father's will
Twas a humbling fulfilling,
that would lead to Calvary's hill.

A life well lived, now bloodied and beaten
For the sins of us all, His body was smitten.

It pleased the Father, to bruise His Son's person
So pleasing this was, from the grave He is risen.

Fulfilling the Father's will,
every dotted i, and every crossed t,
For us He gave His life, paying for all our sin personally.

John 8:46

His Forever Plan

The Lord, the Lord, Yeshua is His Name
You and I His priority, to save is why He came.

To carry out a plan, made before the foundation of the world
Father, Son, Holy Spirit, together God's plan to unfurl.

Holy Spirit upon Mary came, and the Babe began to grow
The Christ Child in Mary's womb,
whom unborn John would know.

In the fullness of the times, Jesus would be born in Bethlehem
The Creator of the Universe,
fulfilling a plan made before time began.

The plan at birth beginning, for 33 years He fulfilled prophecy
The plan almost finished, on a hill called Calvary.

Laid in an empty tomb, a stone to seal the way
Until the morning of day three, an angel rolled the stone away.

Risen from the grave, Jesus secured salvation forever
For all who will believe, a coming day of no more sorrow ever.

Galatians 4:4-5

Smooth with Mercy

To many life is a road, with bumps and potholes plenty
Thank God for trials, to build our faith,
as He smooths our way with mercy.

The bumps still jolt, the potholes still jar
But God shows with mercy, His presence not far.

Along this road, life at times gets tough
In these tough situations,
God always proves to be more than enough.

We can praise God even in the bad, as Job did long ago
For it is in the rough of life,
God's grace and mercy seem most to flow.

Lamentations 3:22-23

Greatly You Are Loved

Not only a little, or just once in awhile
You are greatly loved by God, mile after mile.

Along life's way, there are times our hearts grow weary
It is for times such as these, the Lord cries "Come unto Me!"

Greatly you are loved, in times good or bad
Greatly you are loved, in joyful times or sad.

Greatly you are loved, tattoo it on your brain
Great His love for you, this truth will never change.

Daniel 9:23, 10:11, 10:18-19

Rich in Mercy

Holy, Just, and Righteous is He
God who hates sin, is also rich in mercy.

So rich in mercy, His mercy abounds
So rich in mercy, His mercy astounds.

God rich in mercy, says sin has a great cost
God so rich in mercy, says none need to be lost.

God rich in mercy, says our sin debt must be paid
God so rich in mercy, paid the debt with His sacrifice made.

God so rich in mercy, says, "Come unto Me.",
I have paid your sin debt, with my blood on a tree.

Ephesians 2:4

Image Bearer

Created in God's Image, not as ape, but Man
To walk uprightly with dignity, as only a human being can.

God made the animals first, so many kinds He made
All to be living creatures, of land, air, water and glade.

Then He made a being, apart from all the rest
A being somewhat like Himself,
and place him at Creation's Crest.

Set apart from day six, in the image of his Creator
Man was given dominion over the earth,
and charged to be God's imitator.

Ephesians 5:1

Rejoice Always

Always God is righteous, always God is holy
Never does He change, in Him always there is joy.

Always He is just, always He is true
His eye is on the sparrow, and ever He watches over you.

Never does He slumber, He never ceases to care
He's ever on the lookout, watching over you everywhere.

Always He is everywhere, and always He is good
Always you can go to Him, and always be understood.

Ever He is near you, often in a still small voice
Always when you look to God, there is reason to rejoice!

Philippians 4:4

Nail it to the Cross

Nailed it to the Cross, ALL my sin and shame
Now a new creation, never to be the same.

Healed my heart, healed my hurts, and gave me strength to cope
Renewed my life with purpose, a purpose fueled with hope.

The renewing of my mind; I wish it happened in an instant
But it is often memories of my past,
that keep me from growing distant.

Someday our King will come, and Heaven will come into view
Nothing of sin in our forever home, and a mind cleansed and new!

2 Corinthians 5:17

Let it Go

What is the past, except behind
Especially past failures, that trouble one's mind.

What is past, is past, and cannot be changed
We cannot go backward and redo it again.

We must let it go, or be plagued forever
We can't undo what's been done,
beating ourselves up won't change it ever.

To let it go, is to grasp God's forgiveness
To realize forever, He'll never hold it against us.

No record of our wrongs, to be found in Heaven
Only the reality, we're forever released and forgiven!

Romans 8:1

My Load

Our load is heavy, His burden is light
Insane to bear the burden alone, and it takes all of one's might.

Some burdens are "earned," some burdens just find us
Where they come from matters not, if we keep them they bind us.

Cast our burdens on Him, is the wise thing to do
It is crazy to think, He wants them from you.

He takes our burdens on Him, as He comes along side on the road
Such freedom is realized, Oh! why did I ever keep it my load!

Matthew 11:29-31

Words of Love

The Word of God is His power to create
It is also His power to take and remake.

As the potter remakes from an unshaped mass of clay
God issues His Word to bring change each day.

Holy Spirit indwells to empower and help us understand
He is God's gift to us to help us take hold of God's
commands.

God's commands are not rules to change or enslave us
No!, they are His words of love, to save and to free us!

To live God's will is to live life free
On earth without bondage, and in Heaven eternally!

Romans 9:20-21

A Lamp unto My Feet

A lamp unto my feet, to light the way for me
Showing the way to place my steps, to keep me clean and free.

The world attempts to get me off this path,
with many traps and lures
The Word of God reveals these traps, and keeps my pathway sure.

Prone to wander, from the path, that keeps me close to God
His Word compels my way, and in pursuit of Him, I trod.

A pathway sometimes lined with cares
But always with me, He is there.

His Word a lamp unto my feet,
The nearness of His presence sweet!

Psalm 119:105

Eyes to See

Thank You God for eyes to see, all that You have made
Eyes to see oceans and mountains,
and wonders like the everglades.

Eyes to see with wonder, and move our hearts to praise
Thank you for mountain vistas, from where our eyes can
gaze.

Thank You for the gift of sight, to view Your handiwork
Fill us with awe to praise Your Name, and may this we
never shirk.

Thank You for such variety, in Your wondrous creation
Praise you for its magnificence,
that declares Your glory to every generation!

2 Kings 6:17

Sack of Seed

Oh!, to be a sower, each and every day
To carry a sack of seed, for scattering along our way.

A sack that is full, of many good things
What God gives to us, is our pleasure to bring.

Called to sow, wherever we may go
Seeds of Truth from His Word, that others may know and grow.

Always we can sow, at other times we may get to water
God gets the harvest, and that is what really matters.

We get to sow His seed, in the hearts of all who listen
In hope when we get to Heaven, none of them will be missing!

Psalm 126:5-6

Sing for Joy

Sing for joy a new song, for every day is new
Sound a song of praise, with the settling of the dew.

Sing praises to the Lord, as the sun begins to rise
Sing His exaltation, as it passes through the sky.

Sing Hosanna to the Savior, who saves you from your sin
Sing thanks for the breath you have, as your day begins.

Sing to Him throughout your day, for great things He has done
Sing for joy as your day winds down,
and you rest your night in Him.

Psalm 5:11

Seek the Lord

Seek the Lord while He may be found,
for one day it will be too late
The welcome of Heaven's door,
will be the sealing of hell's gate.

There is freedom from the fires,
in the presence of the Lord
Get off the route of countless souls,
who drifted away from Heaven's shore.

If you seek Him you will find Him, His promises all true
So many times He's called your name,
as He longs to hear from you.

Seek Him now while you can,
Oh!, please call upon His Name
He waits for you with arms of love,
your salvation is why He came.

He took your sin upon His body,
and nailed it to the cross
He covered it there with His blood,
not wanting you forever lost.

Isaiah 55:6

Spiritual Armor

We're in a Battle today, not against flesh and blood
It is the spiritual forces of darkness,
waging war against our Great God.

We have a role to play, we're in the middle of this fight
Though the tide be turned for a time,
God will in the end make all things right.

We live our lives each day, in the midst of so much anger
We carry the Light of Christ,
and go forward in spite of any danger.

We've a witness we must bear, and a message we must share
Forward into battle we go, in the end His victory we'll share.

Ephesians 6:11

Cry of the Unborn

Here I am, in a warm dark place
Well fed and comfortable, but I see no face.

I hear a heart beating, and there is also my own
Not sure what it's about, but for now this is my home.

I am jostled around, as my home moves from place to place
I hear voices outside, but still I see no face.

I can't see where we're going, or where we have been
But I am well cared for in here, in my safe sort of den.

I've been in here for a while now, and today it seems strange
I'm still fed and warm here,
but I sense discomfort and change.

There's a small light in here now,
and something poking around
It seems relentless to find me, but I don't wish to be found!

Poking and reaching, it is me it's trying to get
I can't get away from it, NO!, I am not ready to leave yet...

Psalm 139:13-16 NLT

Jesus is Better

Jesus is better than, the angels God sends to watch over me
Faithful agents that they are. Jesus lives inside of me!

Jesus is better than, the very best this life can give
And when this life is over, forever with Him I'll live!

Jesus is better than, any of the miracles He has done
Even His greatest miracle of all, to save you and me each one!

Jesus is better than, even Heaven itself
After all, what really makes it Heaven,
is Jesus fills it with Himself!

Revelation 21:3

All Must Hear

Oh yes! This is our Father's world
And we've a battle still to fight
So many souls that still need saved
And snatched from their perilous plight.

With our spiritual armor we go forward in love
Shrewd as serpents and gentle as dove.
To share the Gospel as Jesus commands us so
Showing His love as we relentlessly go and go.

We go to find the Wyatts, Dustins, and Sharons
Trusting the Lord to go before, so we can keep on sharing.
Such Good News we have, so good all must hear
May God use our humble sharing, to draw many near.

Romans 10:17

Our Great God

In times of greatest trouble, there is our Great God.
When all seems dark, and hope begins to wane,
there is our Great God.

When all is bad, and bad gets worse, there is our Great God.
When weak, and weary, and struggling badly;
there is our Great God.

When peace comes first, and healing follows;
there is our Great God.
When the struggle is over, and we're relieved and amazed,
Yes! There is our Great God.

Isaiah 45:6

All Things Good

All good things big or small
Tis Jesus Who is Giver of them all.

The day He makes and to us He gives it
Do we think about all He does for us to live it?

From eyes that blink, for sight to remain clear
To the breath He gives us, do we hold these things dear?

Tying our shoes is a simple procedure
Do we think to give God praise for this humble pleasure?

If we complain less and thank God more
We'll anticipate the day as we look for what He has in store.

He is a good God, and even the bad He uses for good reasons
Think of a rough ride on a donkey
to give us such a blessed season!

James 1:17

Bearing Treasure

Our lives are in God's hands
And it is His to make or break our plans.

His ways are not our ways, we're reminded so often
His plans are always best,
and what a blessing to know we're never forgotten.

To be with us forever, wherever we may go
Always working in our lives, how else for others to know?

What a treasure we bear, in these clay jars
We get to take Jesus to others, everywhere they are!

2 Corinthians 4:7

Just a Touch

Free me, o God, from my bondage to sin
Release me please, from chains I placed myself in.

I've been bound so very long; it's cost me so much
I cry out to You, Lord, for deliverance by Your touch.

Just a touch of Your robe, healed a woman long ago
Please touch me Lord Jesus, that freedom I will know.

Touch my heart also, and the hardness remove
Create in me a clean heart, for my life Your love to prove.

Luke 8:45

Come Hear!

With blessings aplenty, and the new mercies we see
As the Gospel we share, and hearts are set free.

We give thanks to the Lord, Who is God up above
And God here below, Who showers us with His love.

One day a trumpet blast we'll hear
As a white horse and rider, come drawing near.

Some will mourn, with hearts buried in fear
But we'll be rejoicing, when the Lord says, "Come here!"

1 Thessalonians 4:16

Christ Our Hope

In every encounter, we try to give hope
Try to pull people off a slippery slope.

We go and go, as Christ goes before
For Him to change lives, forevermore.

Some people come near, some simply say, "Nope!"
Dissuaded we are not, Christ is our hope.

Hearts filled with joy, and minds that soar
For the hope of Heaven, and Jesus to do more.

Colossians 1:27

Held in Awe

Born in a stable, and laid in the straw
Was the only one ever, to be held in awe.

He came on a night, when no one expected
Lived a perfect life, only to be rejected.

The angles knew, the shepherds too
Also, three wise men, and others, a few.

He grew to be questioned, and so often was scorned
A Man of miracles, from Whom life was torn.

Nailed to a cross for the world to see
How ugly our sin, and the price to be free.

He rose from the grave, many more believed
A Babe in a manger, our sin burden relieved.

Matthew 2:11

Delivered

Celebrating the life of Christ, who came to us long ago
Remembering those, who are bound by sin,
and a Savior to whom they can go.

Delivered are we, who sit by a tree,
and toss wrapping to and fro
Delivered are they, who sit in a cell, with no place else to go.

We have our stuff, and family and friends,
to whom our stuff we show
They have a cell, no stuff to show,
but a Savior to whom they can go.

John 1:29

Free to Choose

Free to choose, free to choose, it can be a wonderful thing
A slave I will be, to the choice that I make,
to choose well is a very wise thing.

The Savior to know, or not to know, is mine alone to decide
Eternity, the result of the choice that I make,
to suffer in hell or forever be by Jesus' side.

On a great white horse, He will come for His own,
we'll go to a mansion on a hill
At the judgement seat, He will cast away
all who chose their own will.

Matthew 16:25

Generously Sow

Casting seeds, here and there, everywhere we go
Not our job to be selective, but just to generously sow.

Then to nurture, water, and care;
as a faithful gardener would do
And to watch and pray and go each day,
as the Lord makes each heart new.

A harvest is coming, it's gonna be big; and each of us is a part
One day soon, a trumpet blast, and forever, will finally start!

Matthew 13:3-4a

My Master Before Me

Walking a good road, my Master before me,
and inviting others along
The way is narrow, but always straight,
and on this road one can never go wrong.

The Savior leads and I must follow,
until all my days are through
Then one day, at the end of this road,
I will enter a city where everything is brand new.

I walk this road, my Master before me,
holding out hope and calling to all
Oh please!, come follow Jesus, on the road that is straight
through the gate that is intentionally small.

Matthew 7:13-14

He Paid the Cost

God died on the cross for us,
believe in Him we must
For our sins He paid the cost,
and nailed them to His cross. Ya!

MacKenna Parker Claar (age 6)

1 John 2:2

Year of Our Lord

Each day is the day the Lord has made
Each year the year of our Lord.
We know not what waits for us on the road ahead
But God has blessings there for us,
And knows where each is stored.

Ours is to trust Him for the way,
To follow Him as He leads.
Fixing our eyes on Jesus,
Knowing from sin's curse we are forever freed.

Though the darkness may surround us
And lawlessness may run seemingly unhindered
Jesus sits above the earth in Power
And one day will turn all Man's lawless ways into tinder.

Isaiah 40:22

Never to Relent

Just a heart never satisfied, with what already is done
Always pushing ahead, as if we've only begun.

Tis a heart that first was stirred, so very long ago
And now is growing older, with limited time to go.

So many lives untouched, so little time to find
A fire burning inside, not wanting any left behind.

To go as He has sent, and never to relent
Until His work is done, my race no more to run...

2 Timothy 4:6

His Fruit

Just a bearer of Good News, with a big sack of seed
Sowing here and there, even in between the weeds.

Some grow only to wither, and some don't grow at all
But then there are those who start off slow,
and slowly become tall.

We water with His Word, and nurture all we can
And with a good dose of prayer, fruit begins to grow,
just as He has planned.

The fruit is not to pick, but to display the Master's hand
And show His handiwork, as only His fruit can.

John 15:8

Free

Life is eternal for all who believe
Hell is the same, for all who are deceived.

We preach the news of He who sets hearts free
Others are preachers of a death sentence without a plea.

Someday the Lord will come, and make all things right
For we who follow Him a joy, but for others what a fright.

Jesus is eternal life for believers like you and me
His being eternal is what makes us eternally free!

Matthew 25:46

Downcast to Living

In His yoke together, and together we will go
Go to feed His sheep, and to comfort those who weep.

So many today are lacking rest,
that only the Shepherd can give
Downcast sheep, in a way lost world,
hope draining as if through a sieve.

The Bread of Life who came to die,
for all who are bound by strife
And rose from the grave, victorious He,
with hope for eternal life.

From downcast to living, forgiven and forgiving
In His yoke together with Him, and now forever living.

Matthew 9:36

On the Trail

On the trail, rolling along,
Just following after Him.

The times grow dark, with Truth rejected,
and the near future is looking grim.

But the light of Christ still shines bright,
When one's life is all about Him.

Then one day soon, all will be right
When Christ Jesus comes again!

Luke 5:27

A Matter of Fact

Thanks to be given to creation's Lord
As Satan attacks with his demonic horde.

We continue pursuing the lost by the way
In an old black Ford we chase the highway.

The high way for sure, all should pursue
It's the only way to Heaven, no other will do.

Tis the narrow way found by only a few
So many others want to believe
from "the goo to the zoo to you."

Nothing has happened by Big Bang or chance
Life was created and with it we dance.

No dancing to do without life's Creator,
No Eve to dance with less God made her.

And what is a dance with no one around
And without any light, no one to be found.

Earth is void without God's act
Creation is seriously a matter of fact!

Genesis 1:11

Two Stories as One

With a migratory nature, that stirs my heart each Fall
And a pioneering spirit, prompting me
to respond to God's call.

We plan our way and dream a bit,
as the Lord directs our steps
To keep us on the path He has, for all His plans to fit.

We move from place to place, as our "territory" He expands
And share the Name and Hope of Jesus,
wherever we should land.

A story of His making, two stories told as one
Forty years and counting, the next chapter has begun!

Genesis 2:24; Matthew 19:5

Thankfully Yoked

Just a work in progress, bumping along life's road
Thankful to be yoked with Jesus, His is an easy load.

Wondering what's in store, as life makes another bend
Thankful Jesus always knows,
and we can trust for the where and when.

Not to be unscathed, or spared from all life's pain
Thankful to be yoked with Jesus,
for with Him we need not strain.

For His yoke is easy, and His load is light
Thankful for His leading,
as the road ahead disappears out of sight.

Matthew 11:30

Good News

To a lost and dying world, we go to share Good News
Tis a world without a compass, and so many opposing views.

Good News! Good News! Our lives must speak it so
The Lord has set us each apart to go and go and go.

Someday Jesus is coming back,
with the reality of what's in store
Sure, for us this means Heaven,
but for the lost it means no more...

1 Corinthians 9:16

Let There Be Light

Creation testifies to what only God can do
He created all life, and opened the first zoo.

No primordial soup, boiling for eons of time
But only His spoken Word, and Adam began the line.

Adam's fall was no surprise, God had a perfect plan
Into this sin cursed world, God came in the form of man.

Someday He is coming back, when He'll make all things right
The glory of His being, as God said, "Let there be Light!"

Genesis 1:3

A New Sonrise

There will come a day, when all our work is done
All on earth will be finished, with the coming of the Son.

There is not time to waste, all is moving toward the end
When the Son of God will come, and eternity begins.

The days are passing by, and many can only sigh
But for we who know Him well,
each day a glance toward the sky.

One day a new SONrise will color the sky glorious
As Jesus comes again, and rides the skies victorious!

Luke 1:78-79

Telling

To tell His story anywhere, is a blessed thing to do
Not the audience who matters,
but the hope for things made new.

An audience of One, is ever present with me
His story I get to tell, wherever He will decree.

The setting of my telling, is not what matters most
It is simply to tell the story, in a world desperate for Hope.

My joy is He is listening, a smile on His face
And knowing where I'm telling, is at present the best place!

Luke 2:7

Finally, Finally

What a day it will be, a day like no other
A trumpet and shout, and the coming of our Savior.

His appearing to be, a Sonrise from on high
And for we to be caught up, to meet Him in the sky.

Oh!, glorious day!, soon He will come
And finally, finally, our work on earth will be done!

Titus 2:13

Did We?

This world cannot last, the Lord's trumpet soon will blast
A joyful sound for some,
but mournful for all who will be passed.

News so great we have, news to set hearts and people free
For those who are left behind, tis news that leaves no plea.

Time is running out, His arrival comes with a shout
For all who get to go, did we at least try to let others know?

Matthew 24:40

God's Goodness

Resting in God's goodness, and trusting in His ways
Especially in those times when we need a lot of grace.

Those times when life makes little sense,
and things seem out of whack
God rains His grace upon us,
while the enemy seeks an avenue for attack.

God works His Sovereign will, in providential ways
As we bump along life's road,
and surrender to God ownership of our days.

He doesn't have to make sense,
or give us an explanation
Just remember He truly cares,
and He is God of our salvation!

Isaiah 30:18

Love Relationships

On the road, or face to face
Carrying Jesus' Name all over the place.

A Jesus freak, in love with Him
Love relationships, for Him to begin.

Freedom and peace, for all to know
So great are both, I'm compelled to go.

Go, I do, and tell of Him
Love relationships, for Him to begin!

1 John 4:19

Voice in the Dark

In the armor of God, with Christ before
Together we walk, dark corridors.

Christ and me, with your prayers, we are three
His Name lifted high, the enemy flees.

Hard hearts are many, their mockery flies
The Truth of God, to silence their cries.

Salvation comes to many, if one will only go
Faith comes by hearing, how else will they ever know?

Salvation to work, and hearts made new
A voice in the dark, to many or few...

Luke 3:4

Christ in You

Not always what we share, but just the fact we were there
Christ in us is who they see, Christ in you and Christ in me.

To share is good, to care is more
Present and caring, is a whole lot more.

A bit of hope, for those who have none
Hope of a Savior, and there is only One.

Christ in you, and Christ in me
Unless we go, they will never see!

Matthew 28:20

Love to Others Shared

One day the Lord will come, my hope still holding fast
Today becomes the next, someday my longing will be past.

Heaven really is, and His imminent return equally so
Until the day arrives, I will go and go and go!

What else for me to do? How else to spend my life?
The world around me lost, and filled with so much strife.

Jesus is the answer, Oh!, for all to know
My hope not really hope at all, lest it moves my heart to go.

My going often seems so little, but my going says He cares
And somewhere in His caring, His love to others shared.

John 13:35

Life in Abundance

The path to Heaven is open, for any who wish to go
But the way is lost to many, their sin that makes it so.

Trapped and lost forever, unless someone points the way
'Tis only through the cross, thank God for that wonderful day!

And for we who know it well, great joy is when we tell
For those who don't know at all,
great joy when they hear His call.

To call upon the Lord, and give one's life to Him
To know Him is to love Him,
loving Him is where abundant life begins!

John 10:10

Going

Oh what a Savior!, who bids for all to come
It is His call for all, and not just an invite for some.

But how will they ever hear His voice,
in the midst of all life throws?
His call is heard throughout the earth,
through all who make sure it goes.

The going is the doing, though often the doing isn't seen
But go we must, and go again, far and near and in between.

And as we go, His Word goes too,
and it is this that matters most
It is the going of His Word that grows the heavenly host.

Matthew 28:19

The Lord's Doing

Growing and mentoring and watching them go
It is all the Lord's doing as He makes it so.

He ushers them in and slows them down
They haven't a clue He is readying them,
to one day wear a crown.

We all have a part, as the Lord invites us in
A life placed where they are safe, a new life work to begin.

Oh!, what a joy to introduce them to Jesus!
We just keep sharing His Word,
and our love for Him He uses.

One day He will call us all home to Him
The life works completed, and eternity begins!

John 15:16

More to See

"Come on!, come on!", the Lord says to me
"There is much more to do, and much more to see!"

Calling me forward, toward an eternal destiny
Forever with Him, and in Him forever free.

One short life to live, as if a whiff of smoke
But then eternal life with Him,
He is the Lord of Heaven's host.

Together we travel, with Him in the lead
And me in tow, me whom He freed.

The chains of the past, all broken for me
To run after Him, forever set free!

John 1:50

Remember the Prisoners

"Remember the prisoners", God's Word says
"As if you were with them", think hard that it is.

Locked up in a strange place, with many others like you
All wanting to go free, but relatively few do.

Day after day, the routine is the same
And the crowd that is like you,
well they might drive you insane.

But into this dark place, your prayers are free to go
There is the Word of God also, and Holy Spirit sows.

Remembering them, you pray for their freedom
Freedom from so much,
as God begins His work to redeem them.

Once so very guilty of sin, you and I should have died
But our freedom was won, only when to Jesus we cried.

Their freedom also, hangs with them in the balance
Cry to Jesus as we did, He is God of another chance.

Hebrews 13:3

How Marvelous

How marvelous, how wonderful,
the return of Jesus our Lord will be
Someday, we'll all be in glory,
with a multitude He alone could set free.

And to be numbered among them,
a thought too wonderful for me
But, there I am, and there you are,
and together Jesus' face we will see.

How marvelous, how wonderful,
a multitude as vast as the seas
And to think that Jesus allowed us
a small part in setting a few of them free.

Revelation 20:15

Creation Groaning

The sun goes down and darkness reigns,
but Light comes in the morning
Winter blasts with frigid cold,
all Creation seems to groaning.

Winter comes and winter goes,
new life always follows
Trees are bare, the days are shorter,
but there is ever hope with tomorrow.

Such it is, from life to death to life again;
as season ends and season begins
There is always hope of something more,
a day when life will be without end.

In the winter of life things slow to a crawl,
the days grow few and "is this all?"
But here is His person, and hear His voice,
"Time to go, I've come to call."

Darkness fades, the sun shines in,
winter is over and new life begins
To breathe earth's last, is to inhale Heaven;
and behold, the God of life without end.

Romans 8:22-23

God Freely Gave

The gift of His Son, God freely gave
In hope the souls of us all would be saved.

He came and lived, and gave, and gave
Then to a cross, and a rich man's grave.

Though destined for death, death on Him had no hold
He rose Victor from the grave, just as He told.

Out of the grave, and up in the sky
To take His place, and reign from on high.

The day fast approaching, when He will come again
And take us away to the promised land!

John 10:18

Manger and the Cross

Rejoice!, Rejoice!. God has come to save
To Bethlehem and a manger, in a dry and dusty cave.

So glorious His being, so humbly did he grow
Humble to the cross, where God's love for us most showed.

The cross without the manger, no, this could never be
The manger without the cross, and none could ever be free.

Luke 4:18-19

Christmas 2020

It is Christmas 2020, who'd have ever thought
Way back in the day, with my life a mess,
this would be how far I got?

Sixty-two years old now, and God willing,
many more years to go
Though along my way to get here,
I was so often tossed to and fro.

The tossing ended one day, some thirty years ago
When God decided "Enough!",
it was time for the old me to go.

Christmas time is here again,
and I can't help but grin and grin
Along came Jesus to take my hand,
a brand-new life with Him to begin!

2 Corinthians 5:17

Leave the Past Behind

For years and years I lived in the past with all its "What If?"
Thinking my life was wasted, believing the devil's myth.

For sure, I wish I would have acted differently,
and not wasted what I had
So much that might have been,
but dwelling in the past is bad.

Your past will wear you down,
if you continue going there often
It is an anchor keeping you from growing,
and will never allow you to blossom.

God has so much more for you,
if you will surrender all to Him
He is God who redeems your past,
oh please invite Him in.

Your past will still be your past,
but it will become a story of your redemption
God will forgive and bless,
when you cry to Jesus for salvation.

No more devil's lies, the Truth of God's Word will set you free
God will be working in your life,
as He readies you for eternity.

John 12:26

Wedding Supper

A wedding feast so great, a celebration so very grand
It will be the celebration for the Wedding Supper of the Lamb.

Sins forever gone, and time will be no more
Far beyond our imagination, all that He has in store.
For sure one day He is coming,
for sure it is for we who follow Him
For sure with Him forever, all our toil on earth is done!

Revelation 19:9

Charging

Charging on the gates of hell, until all our strength is gone
While looking to our Lord, for more strength to carry on.

The enemy is relentless, so we must also be
Our relentlessness God uses in His plan to set souls free.

Sometimes these bones grow weary,
as our charge becomes a grind
But it is the Shepherd's grand plan,
that no sheep are left behind.

Charging the gates of hell,
with the renewed strength He gives
All His sheep to be in Heaven,
together with Him to forever live!

Matthew 16:18

Thankful

Thankful for a Savior who came and died for me
Thankful He gave Himself up and laid upon a tree.

Thankful my sin upon His body He took
Thankful He paid the debt I owed,
and thankful my name is recorded in His book.

Thankful He loved me so much then,
thankful He loves me so much still
Thankful He took my sin
and suffered for me on Calvary's hill.

Thankful my sin He buried in a grave not my own
Thankful I am His,
and one day He'll come and take me home!

1 Thessalonians 5:18

Shepherds and Sheep

His heart is for His sheep, and shepherds He has called
To care for and feed His sheep,
and keep them from getting mauled.

Wolves are all about, looking to steal some sheep
A staff and rod are the Shepherd's tools,
and the sheep are His to keep.

Undershepherds He has sent, to be His hands and feet
To drive the wolves away, and to care for and feed His sheep.

One day the Chief Shepherd comes to gather all His own
it will be the Shepherd's peace
to be gathered with them and going home.

1 Peter 5:2

All Will Be Told

The going isn't easy, nor did He say it'd be
But strength is guaranteed, when it is to Him we flee.

So many this day would perish,
should God's judgement unfold
We go, and go, and go; in hope that all will be told.

Though many may not listen, our task is to go and tell
And to do the most we can, to get folks off the road to hell.

We've a Savior who paid the price, with His priceless sacrifice
His return will be without warning,
like a thief who comes at night!

1 Timothy 2:3-4

Hold Up the Cross

For the love of Christ I go
His love for others to show.

To hold up the cross of the Savior who died
To tell of His love and why He gave Himself to be crucified.

The joy before Him, millions untold
One sheep at a time, brought into His fold.

I can only keep going and doing what I can
While holding Him high, God's Perfect Lamb!

John 3:15-16

Enough

Our road is often bumpy and sometimes downright rough
But the Lord is always faithful, and always provides enough.

Enough to keep us going, enough to open doors
Enough to offer hope, enough to heal the sores.

Our part is really simple, just go and go and go
And in our faithfulness to go,
the presence of Christ does glow.

2 Corinthians 12:9

Your Ransom is Paid

The task is simple, His Word to proclaim
To preach His Good News, again and again.

Success isn't how many surrender,
or perhaps even how many hear
What matters is sharing with hope and no fear.

The results are His doing, His doing uses our sharing
His command is to "Go!", and going is daring.

It is to be of good courage, and courage the heart of His care
Care that is visible; are heart filled with hope
and the absence of fear.

Near to Him, no need to be afraid
From His presence we call, "Your ransom is paid!"

1 Timothy 2:5-6

Each by Name

He calls them each by name,
though billions and billions they are
And holds them all in His hands,
though they are spread so very far.

Stars so many, and most quite large
They're to point us to the Creator,
from Whom they get their charge.

A God so very BIG, and we so very small
Seven and a half billion we are, and Jesus knows us all.

Some day He will ride on high,
on a white horse past the stars
It will be to come for us,
who have made the Savior ours!

Psalm 147:4

Keep Going

"Go!", says my Lord to one such as I
And make as you go, those who follow I.

"Go!", and relentlessly tell them how to come
And while you are telling, show them how it's done.

The road is simple and I am up ahead
Follow after Me, bringing others who need to be fed.

"I AM the Good Shepherd", says Jesus to His sheep
My sheep are yours to care for, but they are My sheep
and mine alone to keep.

"Go!", and keep going, no matter what comes your way
Know that I AM with you every step of every day.

One day your task on earth, will finally reach its end
I will come to get you for your eternity to begin

1 Corinthians 9:16

Object of His Love

What am I in the scheme of a cosmos so very grand?
The Universe is so vast, and I am a mere speck of sand.

Creation was made for beings such as I
I see the greatness of my God in the vastness of the night sky.

Creation cries to me, "You have a God who so much cares!"
Nowhere I can escape, everywhere His creation shares.

Who am I but the object of His love
So great His love for me, He came down from above.

Forever I am His, His face one day I'll see
Each day I live my life embraced in His love for me!

Psalm 17:8

Relentless Pursuit

Once a fool, lost in sin, no room for Jesus, not wanting Him in
An insane way to live one's life,
a sure-fire way to live in strife.

No relief apart from God, run if you will,
but where will you trod?
Reality is He made the sod, wherever one runs, there is God.

Not getting away, or ever escaping,
His relentless pursuit is ever shaking
To make one His own is what He desires,
from this pursuit He never tires.

The day will come when one breathes his last,
no way to escape, death comes fast
Oh what will become of His relentless pursuit,
Hell for a fool or heavenly fruit?

Hebrews 13:5

Better is One Day

Better is one day with the Lord together on the way
Side by side, each step to take, to experience His day.

To think one day this will be forever,
with nothing ever again to draw us away.
But by His side eternally as we walk along the way.

It is all because of Him, He has such great love for you
One day we will breathe our last on earth,
and inhale Heaven new.

Psalm 84:10

Day of Reckoning

The day is fast approaching when time will be no more
The signs are all around, earthquakes, lawlessness,
and rumors of war.

A day of judgement for many, a day of reckoning for all
The Day that will bring an end, to the time of Adam's fall.

A day not pleasant for some, but a day so long ago foretold
A day swiftly approaching,
and a time for the Church to be bold.

Romans 13:12

There Will Come a Day

There will come a day when time will be no more
A day when the things of earth have passed,
and we arrive at heaven's door.

Oh for the bliss of eternity to come
And oh for the peace when our work on earth is done.

Eternity with Jesus, and all who know Him well
A joy so overwhelming, no one can really tell.

To be home with Him forever, in a far, far, better place
All the pains and sorrows of earth,
forever gone, without a trace.

Revelation 21:5

The Day Approaches

The sun shines bright, the mountains testify, God is in control
So many voices, so much chaos,
is the last bell beginning to toll?

The world in turmoil, the speech of many is proof;
but God remains in control
The day will come, when the Son will rise,
and the universe will be rolled up like a scroll.

For now we wait, the news is often bad,
and the bell continues to toll.
But the Day approaches, when time will end,
and the King comes to take us home.

Ephesians 5:16

New Things

A new thing God does, every now and then
He doesn't give a warning, and we're never knowing when.

Sometimes He heals a body, and one is cancer free
Sometimes He makes a way, so one is able to flee.

There are times the insurmountable seems to come to stay
Only for God to show His power
and insurmountable goes away.

He has a plan for you, to prosper and not harm
He's on the way ahead, the devil to disarm.

His plans are always good, He knows the way for you to take
He's always thinking of you, and the surprise He will make.

Isaiah 43:19

Floods with His Mercy

His mercy is offered to all for free
Some foolishly reject it, while others receive it with glee.

'Tis a humbling thing to realize one's need
A gracious thing to be immersed in God's mercy
and from burdens freed.

God gives grace to the humble while He opposes the proud
Narrow the way that leads to God's mercy,
or proudly one can stick with the crowd.

Being washed in Christ's blood, as God floods with His mercy
Is to experience God's blessings on a Spirit filled journey.

Mark 15:38; Hebrews 10:20

You Do, Jesus

Nobody loves me like You do, Jesus
Nobody knows me the way You do.

Nobody loves me like You do, Jesus
Nobody guards my heart like You do.

Nobody loves me like You do, Jesus
Nobody else understands me through and through.

Nobody loves me like You do, Jesus
Nobody else owns my heart like You.

Nobody loves me like You do, Jesus
Nobody can keep me from loving You!

1 John 3:1

Peace is a Person

The world lacks peace, and rightfully so,
"Tis futile so much humanity pursues.
So many have answers, so many are wrong
Only One holds all that is true.

We run here and there, to chase this and that
All the while He waits to be found.
Like dogs chasing tails, we wear ourselves out
But continue to go 'round and 'round.

Peace is lacking, but is there for the asking
If only we'd slow down and see.
Peace is a person, Truth is the same,
Christ Jesus, it is He!

John 16:33

Heaven is Open

Invite the worst we must; and the best?
Yes, we must invite them too
None are beyond redemption,
unless we decide Heaven has room for only a few.

Who do we pass by so many each day,
with nary a word said or offering a clue
Do we really believe Heaven is open to all,
or it is only reserved for a select few?

Jesus saved me, vile as I was,
and my life mostly saying pee-yew!
Reality is, compared to Christ, the same can be said of you.

Humbling it is, and perhaps hard to face,
but oh, it is so very true
Humbled now, with nothing to lose,
we've got a lot of work to do.

All people are equal at the foot of His cross
We're commanded to go, a message to share,
in hope to reach the lost.

Revelation 22:7

So Many

The harvest time has come, with eternity in view
But will it be a harvest of many, or so very few.

The harvest doesn't happen, unless seeds of truth are cast
But the time for casting seeds is passing very fast.

The workers are so few, and yet so many need to know
In times such as we are in, so many need to go.

it is time for the church to rise, and to answer Jesus' call
Or will we continue our slumber, and allow the many to fall?

Ezekiel 33:6

Shoes to Share

Some plant, some water, some get to bring in the harvest
The vineyard is His, the fruit is too,
it matters not whose harvest is largest.

What pleasure to share in Master's work,
and a joy it is He who invites us
Serving together 'neath His watchful care, well it is just real delight.

Some are givers, some are prayers,
some are goers who need the other two
Prayers and gifts together place the goer in Gospel shoes.

Shoes to share on feet to go, in great part because of you
For these shoes and so much more,
missionaries thank the Lord for you!

Ephesians 6:15, TLB

Place of Peace

Onward, forward, we must go
How else for the lost to ever know?

The enemy rages, lawlessness grows
The light of the gospel continues to glow.

We hold up Christ, and go with hope
To a much confused world, so many unable to cope.

Onward, forward, we must go
With Christ before us, and His love to show.

Crazy times these are, scary times for some
Jesus is the place of peace, through us He bids them, "Come!"

Hebrews 4:9

Weeping and Rejoicing

Hope filled hearts
On our way
Along life's paths
Minds to sway.

Sometimes a march
Sometimes a trot
Seeking the downcast
And those distraught.

Weeping with some
Rejoicing with others
Sharing with all
Our loving Father.

Calling and calling
Won't you come
Noise to many
Peace for some.

Romans 12:15

Green Pastures

The Good Shepherd promises green pastures for us to take a rest
He is ever faithful to lead us, as we go about our quest.

To go and share the Gospel, He is always there before
He is on the road ahead, knowing fully what's in store.

The joy of sharing Jesus, the pleasure of watching seeds take root
We give of what He has given, watching Him we follow suit.

To pray and share the Gospel, and make disciples too
We join the Master in His work,
as he makes souls and lives brand new.

Along the way as we go, we're in the Master's care
He plans our restful places, and has green pastures waiting there.

Our spiritual eyes He opens, so we don't miss the green
As we till heart soil for planting, His provision for us is often seen.

Psalm 23:2

Investing in Others

Investing in others, as the Lord provides and leads
Watching people grow after they're freed.

Then parting ways, with a bit of remorse
But resting in Jesus, who providentially steers their course.

The gospel spreads as we go our separate ways
The Light of Christ also, He walks beside us all our days.

To not grow weary, and to keep doing good
Just seizing opportunities, to do what we could.

Galatians 6:9

Surrender

Surrender is key to all God wishes to give
Couple this with obedience, for how God would have us live.

Surender is a heart, wide open to the Lord
Obedience demonstrates our love for Him,
as we live according to His Word.

Good things He has planned, for us to experience and do
Blessings aplenty to come our way,
an abundance of mercy and grace too.

Best of all is His presence with us, wherever He will lead
As we surrender to His will, and walk with Him forever free.

Psalm 1:3

Only a Babe?

Just a tiny babe, lying in a manger
Angels looking on in amazement and wonder.

The planets and stars He made, looking down where He laid
Now lying in a manger, by His Creation arrayed.

Even a star, never seen before or since
Stood over its Creator, to provide the world a glimpse.

His glory was exposed, in so many ways;
Angels and stars, yet, He was lying on the hay.

Unfathomable to think, He would come to us this way,
He who spoke Creation into being,
is He who brought us Christmas day!

1 Corinthians 8:6

Knit for a Purpose

My life knit together in darkness by the Creator
Knit with purpose, specifics, and a plan for my future.

Good works He planned for me, before Able was ever born
With these works in mind, He carefully knit my form.

Then came the day, as a little person I arrived
Many rough years ahead, but by His hand I survived.

Lots of bumps on my life road, and even a crash or three
All the while God calling my name,
to a place where He would set me free.

At the end of my rope, from out of the darkness,
I stepped into His marvelous Light
He took away my sinful blindness,
and gave me spiritual sight.

Eyes now open, seeing Him,
knowing for a wretch like me He came
From such darkness He delivered me,
to one day write of His glory and fame!

Proverbs 19:21

Only God

Humble beginnings, the son of a truck driver
A blue-collar family, with blue-collar neighbors.

A very wild child, so often in trouble
A rebellious teen, so much promise, but reduced to rubble.

A loud and angry man, bent toward rage, and buried in sin
Wanting so badly to be different,
but chained to his past, unable to begin.

A praying mother, and a praying wife,
Joined by others; asking God to change another life.

Hurts and anger, unable to cope,
a mind filled with garbage, without any hope
God had a plan, He continued pursuit,
and waited for a life to run out of rope.

So many gave up, and from him turned away;
alone and distraught, he continued to plod
Feeling lost and alone, and crying for help;
looked up from his pit, and there was God.

Only God can save, and cleanse, and restore such a life
Only God can hold, and heal,
and put to rest such anger and strife.

Only God can make a new creation,
from a life so very flawed
Only God can make a new you; only God, only God!
2 Corinthians 5:17

Untamable God

The untamable God, all powerful is He
The Lion of Judah, on the move and roaming free.

He encompasses the Universe, and answers to none
Powerful, Holy, Eternal, and full of mercy; there is only One.

His throne in the heavens, He does as He pleases
Always He is good, His love never ceases.

He reigns Supreme, and shows grace to all
On righteous and unrighteous, He causes the rain to fall.

He has life in Himself, and is also Life Giver
His sacrifice for all, He is also Forgiver.

He is a just God, who must punish all sin
He came, and He died, and came back to Life again.

Sin had no hold on Him, nor did the grave
The untamable God, forever He saves.

Exodus 19:16

No Beginning or End

God is self-existent, without beginning is He
Alive without end, Father of eternity.

He is Alpha and Omega, the Beginning and the End
So awesome is He, no mind can fully comprehend.

He is the Timeless One, Who exists outside of time
Ever full of mercy, forever He is kind.

Time is in His hands, He sees past and future as present
He fills all space and time, and alone is Omnipresent.

Infinite is He, and forever His reign extends
He is the Ancient of Days, with no beginning and no end.

Revelation 4:8

A Big God

A great big God, who spoke Creation into being
With a bang He spoke into the darkness,
and in six days life was happening.

Out of nothing something came, a thing only God can do
Humanity and Satan try, but only God creates life,
including you.

A God so big, He can make the sun stand still
He keeps the Universe in order, by the power of His will.

Not a sparrow falls to the ground,
without His knowing where and when
It is He who makes the rainbow; Noah's flood He did send.

He decided to be both God and man,
and to earth one day He came
On the cross He paid for all humanity's sin,
desiring our endless souls to claim.

One day He'll roll the Universe up like a scroll,
and create heaven and earth new
His own to live with Him forever, before time began,
each one of us He knew.

Deuteronomy 10:17

All My Sin

All my sin, on His body laid
He did no wrong, had no debt to be paid.

Ever Righteous is He, in word, thought, and deed
He owed not the wages of sin, from which to be freed.

A train load of sin, I did own
A mountain of debt, I did owe.

He called for my sin, and I gave it all to Him
It was the punishment due me, that did Him in.

My debt was so massive, by me it could never be paid
He owed no debt, but for my freedom, His sacrifice He made.

There on the cross, He died for me
There in the grave, He buried my sin for eternity.

Jeremiah 33:8

Glory of the Lord

One day Jesus will come, and in His presence we will be
All our mental pictures fail, when all His glory we shall see.

Risen from the earth, to meet Him in the air
When we see Him we'll be like Him,
and in all His glory share.

Oh to be like Jesus!, with sinless eyes and pure minds
In the presence of His glory, and no longer bound by time.

Forever to be with Jesus, forever all there acting like He
Forever praising His Name,
forever overwhelmed by His glory.

2 Chronicles 7:3

Cheerful Investing

We've a hope that will last forever in an Eternal Savior
So much for us He has done,
giving back to Him is a pleasure.

"You can't outgive God!", so many have cried
Blessings in abundance, for all who have tried.

Cheerful giving, is what please God;
not the amount that matters, for God looks at the heart.
Joyfully giving, from all God gives;
promised blessings in return, a cheerful offering is the start.

God invites us to test Him in only this;
this testing is backed by promises He gives.
A return running over, for Kingdom investments;
capped by a "Well done!" only He can give!

Luke 6:38

Very Best News

Going relentlessly, He commands us to go
Hoping and praying for all who hear to know.

To know Jesus is to know His great love
Humbled by His sacrifice, realizing He left His home above.

He was not obligated to give His life for ours
He proved His love upon the cross,
paid for all our sin and gladly bears the scars.

The Gospel is the very best news anyone can ever hear
With Christ going before us,
we share the Gospel without fear.

The very best thing a Christ follower can do
Is tell the story of Jesus,
so others can one day go to Heaven too!

John 4:28-29

Eyes of Hope

By faith we go to the lost in dark places
With eyes of hope, we see the grief in their faces.

By faith we see a life to be changed
We share Jesus' love, and pray for Him to break their chains.

Forsaken by so many, their lives in shambles
Encouraging them to take Jesus' hand,
and assuring them it is no gamble.

Jesus wants them for His own,
to make them part of His family
To bless their lives with good things,
and spare them from further calamity.

John 8:10-11

What Matters Most

The battle is fierce and the storms are raging
But the Giver of Life is still active and engaging.

In the midst of growing darkness, His light still prevails
The Word of God goes forth, and His Word never fails.

Our purpose here on earth is clear, it's to be "salt and light"
To be so much like Jesus, we're seen to be a peculiar sight.

It's easier to shine, with the world plunging into darkness
Our lives create a thirst for Him,
as the world grows more faithless.

The day is fast approaching, when Jesus will come again
In the end what matters most,
is that we lived our lives for Him.

Luke 19:16

Our Companion

Going and going, with God's Word in hand
To a motley crew and renegade band.

A burning desire for all to know
A heart for sowing seeds and watching them grow.

Taking the Lord with us as we go here and there
He promises to be our companion,
every day, and everywhere.

To go each day with Jesus, life with Him is an adventure
Abundant life He promises,
all that is required is our surrender.

Deuteronomy 30:8

Jehovah Jireh

Jehovah Jireh, our Faithful and Trustworthy Provider
Grace, mercy, compassion, and caring,
help make up His character.

So many attributes, so many things to praise Him for
He is Awesome, Fearsome, Magnificent, Glorious, Holy,
and so much more.

No attribute to put above another,
He is all, all at the same time
What if He were all the others,
but not caring, gracious, merciful, and kind?

God's provision is huge, creating us aside,
without His provision, none would survive
Survival is important, but life is much more,
His provision allows us, also to be kind.

And not just kind, but merciful, gracious, caring, and more;
allowing us to provide.
Jehovah Jireh, our Provider; allowing us a part in His plan,
as He keeps us well supplied.

Genesis 22:14

Imitators

To imitate God, His children we are,
and imitate Him we should
Perfectly love, perfectly kind, to act like God is good.

Merciful, gracious, and compassionate is He;
it is great when we are all three
God is well pleased, when we imitate Him;
His character for others to see.

When folks watch us, they should see our Father,
and see that we are His
They may not know it, when they see it;
He shapes into His likeness, for such a time as this.

Imitators of God, as dearly loved children,
so His goodness others can see
It is His goodness that leads to repentance,
and repentance is what sets hearts free.

At the end of the day, if we did a good job, God is glorified
To glorify God is a blessed thing,
and it shows we walk close to His side.

Galatians 5:1

God is Good

God is good and He does good, He cannot do otherwise
All He does is somehow good, and good is also right.

His goodness is seen in so many ways,
including His plans for our days
His plans are to prosper and not to harm,
with our lives He never plays.

His goodness is with us all the time,
even in times of discipline
It is for our good He disciplines,
and it is His goodness that brings our correction.

It is His goodness, and not a hard hand,
that leads us to repentance
It is also His goodness, that never gives up,
and gives us another chance.

Such a good God, showing kindness and patience,
drawing us ever closer to Him
Our lives to be clean, our character good,
and our souls filled with His goodness to the brim!

Romans 2:4

About the Author

Randy was born and raised in Phoenix, Arizona, and married his high school sweetheart, Rhonda. They have 3 children and 9 grandchildren. In 1987 the family moved to Bagdad, Arizona, where Randy worked as a hard rock miner for 14 years. In 1995 God called Randy to ministry and Randy began preaching and teaching, including serving for a year as interim pastor of a small community church. In 1999, surrendering to God's leading, they moved to central Illinois where Randy worked as an ironworker and continued to pursue ministry. After his ordination, he and Rhonda joined InFaith, (InFaith.org), and in 2003 were assigned to the mission field in Southern Arizona. Since then Randy and Rhonda have served with InFaith in north central Arizona where Randy currently serves as Chaplain for the Yavapai County Detention facilities. Randy and Rhonda live on a mini farm in the Verde Valley where they raise their ten-year-old little girl MacKenna and enjoy various outdoor activities that include, fishing, hunting, wood cutting, and four wheeling. Randy continues to have a passion for ministry, sharing the Gospel, making a difference in the lives of others, and of course, writing. He finds nothing more fulfilling than using his God-given gifts to demonstrate the true freedom that surrender, obedience, and faith in our relationship with the Lord Jesus Christ brings.

Randy would love to hear from his readers. You may contact him by email at azgrizzly59@gmail.com

Made in the USA
Middletown, DE
23 December 2021

56946926R00135